Praise for *How To Focus On Success!* by Roy Saunderson

"This is an extremely helpful book that shows you how to focus and concentrate on achieving the most important goals in your life. It is an invaluable success tool for every ambitious person!"

BRIAN TRACY
Author, *Maximum Achievement*

"This practical guide for focusing says it clearly and effectively. A valuable tool for those who know they are often scattered in their efforts despite their inner desire to get it done."

ROSITA PEREZ, CPAE
President, Creative Living Programs, Inc.

"This book is a real treasure chest of useful and effective success techniques."

JACK CANFIELD
Co-author, *Chicken Soup for the Soul*

"This is a book written with heart, by a man with heart. His honesty and insights will help you on the path to your own success."

REVA NELSON
Speaker and author of *Risk It!* and *Bounce Back!*

"Focus is the key to growing a more successful life and Roy's book is full of the key questions designed to get you there!"

TOM STOYAN
Canada's Sales Coach

"Most people spend more time planning their summer vacation than the rest of their lives. This book by Roy Saunderson will help you to focus on what you want and how to get it."

PATRICIA FRIPP, CPAE
Author, *Get What You Want* and Past President
National Speakers Association

"A "must read"! Roy Saunderson takes you by the hand and shows you the "how" of developing FOCUS."
JAMES F. HENNIG, PhD
Professional Speaker and Past President
National Speakers Association

"These pages are a wealth of challenge to "become" and "to be" through a journey of focus, determination, action and results!"
NAOMI RHODE, CSP, CPAE
Professional Speaker, Author, and Past President
National Speakers Association

"Insightful and motivating! Roy speaks from experience in his book How To Focus On Success! *in such a way that everyone will benefit by reading it immediately and making it a part of their personal library."*
ART BERG, CSP
Professional Speaker and Author

"Roy's generosity of spirit—so evident to those who know him—comes through in the printed word. This book will make a difference in the life of any who invest in themselves and read it."
ALAN SIMMONS, CSP
Professional Speaker and Author
Member of the Canadian Speaking Hall of Fame

How To *Focus* On Success!

Create a laser-like focus
for achieving your success

ROY SAUNDERSON

Recognition Management Institute
London, Ontario, Canada

Canadian Cataloguing in Publication Data

Saunderson, Roy,
   How to focus on success!: creating a laser-like focus for achieving your success

ISBN 0-9681767-0-4

   1. Achievement motivation.. 2. Self-actualization (Psychology) 3. Motivation (Psychology) 4. Success.
I. Recognition Management Institute (London, Ont.)
II. Title

BF637.S8S28 1997   158'.1   C97-900045-9

Use of the names Kodak, Fuji and Minolta are made with permission.

Cover Design: Walter Sayers, Stainless Steele Communications
Printer: Webcom Limited
Cover Photo: James Hockings

How to Order

Single copies can be ordered from your favourite bookstore or with shipping and handling from the Recognition Management Institute, 635 Southdale Road East, Suite 180, London, Ontario Canada, N6E 3W6; telephone (519) 685-0564. See order form at back of book. Quantity discounts are also available. On your letterhead, include information concerning the intended use of the books and the number of books you wish to purchase.

Acknowledgments

This has to be one of the hardest yet most enjoyable parts of writing a book.

Why the hardest? Because it really makes you stop and think about all the people who have helped make you what you are today. They surely deserve a few kudos for their influence and guidance upon the writer of this book. And then it is doubly hard because you don't want to miss anyone either. So to all the friends, teachers, employers, professors, colleagues, and family, thank you for touching my life.

At the same time, the act of thinking of all the wonderful people who have made a difference to me personally, and contributed to this book in whatever way they have, brings nothing but joy and gratitude to my heart and soul.

My Mum and Dad have taught me the value of hard work, which I needed to focus on when working at all kinds of odd hours on this book. One definition of a successful person is someone who does things that need to be done even when they don't want to. Welcome to the truth about parenthood. Thanks, Mum and Dad.

I am so grateful I discovered the library. I remember being scared to ask my parents' permission to go and get my own library card and go by myself. My fear of asking was self-imposed, and once I broke the barrier, so began a love affair with books and long visits to the library. Much gratitude and thankfulness is expressed to the late Dr. Norman Vincent Peale, whose book *The Power of Positive Thinking* changed my life during my childhood. I never met him, but I feel I know him.

My adult life has been influenced by the great motivators and authors of the twentieth century. Where would I be without the help of Denis Waitley, Stephen Covey, Brian Tracy, Tom Peters, Les Brown, Jim Rohn, Mark Victor

Hansen, Jack Canfield, Anthony Robbins, Leo Buscaglia, Kenneth Blanchard, and the world's greatest motivational writer, the late Og Mandino. To each of you my heartfelt thanks and appreciation for the work, time, effort and gifts you have shared through your writings.

And then there are the many professional speakers that have inspired me along the way to getting into this giving profession. Besides all of the above authors who are also exceptional speakers, I would like to thank several key people. Alan Simmons spoke at my first ever chapter meeting that I attended of the National Speakers Association in Toronto, and has acted as a mentor en route to where I am today. He always asked me when was I going to make up my mind about going full time. Here's to you Alan.

Susan Duxter was a great support in getting me linked with the bureau business, and referring me to my first out of province engagement. Barbara Kincaide for believing in me when I was just starting in the speaking business. Betty Ann van Gastel for keeping me going and listening to some tears when providence lined up my first two major engagements.

To the many top-notch speakers I have called and written and who have offered ideas and sent materials that I could learn from them. Thanks to Jim Pancereo, Shep Hyken, Bill Brooks, Liz Curtis Higgs, and Marjorie Brody. Special thanks to Art Berg. Congratulations on earning your C.S.P. (Certified Speaking Professional).

For the incredible and giving, support and suggestions from all the speakers who attended the 1996 National Speakers Association convention in Orlando, Florida. These include none other than Tom Stoyan, all the way from Canada, who in his loving and sharing manner still got me to focus on getting out there and speaking as we met in the convention hallways. No wonder you're Canada's Sales Coach. For Les Brown, who decked out in a Mickey Mouse T-shirt and shorts, spent twenty minutes of quality time sharing from his experience. That meant so much to me. Thanks, Les. To Tony Alessandra who has added to my business; Rosita Perez who always touches my heart, and reminds me that everything is "small stuff"; Patricia Fripp whose talk at Toastmasters International got me keynoting before I knew what I was doing; Brian Tracy who helped me again in setting focused goals and indirectly helped me get our first house; Jim Rohn the master conveyor of wisdom who got me thinking; and all who spoke and gave themselves away, for free.

The final speaker I must thank is Larry Winget. I did not attend his session at the 1996 NSA convention. But as I lined up to buy some audiotapes someone behind me said you should *really* get Larry's session on tape. I am glad I did. Without his profound questioning of *"if you believe in yourself, and your message and your audience, how come you don't have any product for them to take some of you away with them?"*, this book would never have started. Now I have an audiotape, and a book written. Thanks for reminding me that belief makes the impossible become possible.

Thanks to Janine Foster for graciously agreeing to plow through and edit the original manuscript.

There are some wonderful children who have to put up with their Dad's corny sense of humour; his continual learning of patience through their tutelage; getting used to him being at work at home; bearing with their life experiences being shared publicly with others to grow from and laugh with; and being the greatest audience a speaker could ever have. A big hug and kiss to all of you Marjorie, Tisha, Andrew, Camille and Kyle.

To my best friend who has believed in me from the beginning. You have traveled some unlikely paths and stayed put when you would rather travel. You have encouraged me to do what I believed was right when everyone else thinks you're crazy. You have given me five, beautiful children and made each house we have lived in a home. You knew this book could be written before it was even thought of. You make everything worthwhile. Know that I love you tons. Thanks, Irene.

CONTENTS

INTRODUCTION

As the father of five wonderful children, I have had the privilege of being present and assisting in the delivery at each of their births. After the long burden of carrying each of these children to full term, my dear wife has had to bear with the significant pains of labor, often with significant risk of life, to allow each of our children to have a successful introduction into this mortal world.

To hold a newborn infant is an incredible experience. To have been a part of this amazing creation process, and now to see each one of them as they pursue their own paths towards success, is a unique and treasured experience.

Writing this book has been another creative process that I would never have imagined possible. Its development was far from a burden as I relived the different life events to share with you. There was only joy as I realized what a wonderful life I have been blessed with. Each page allowed me to gain greater courage to write more on how you can focus on success. And now you are holding in your hand a bundle of joy that I have given birth to. Another successful introduction.

What I do know is that as you apply some of the principles covered in this book, you will have the pleasure of seeing your own birth of whatever area of success you have set goals for yourself to achieve.

During these past years of living my life, I have learned that there is one thing that will help you and I achieve all of the health, wealth, relationships, position, fame and the accomplishments that we want in life more than anything else. That one thing is simply to *focus*.

It's a simple fact that if you focus a camera, binoculars, telescope or even a microscope, you will see life much more clearly.

Throughout this book I have reflected on things that have happened in my life when I stumbled upon the idea of focusing. I say stumble because on many occasions I didn't even know I was doing it.

Being a little older and wiser I am now discovering that I need to learn from these isolated experiences and apply what I have learned on a consistent basis. Every time I have focused on the various skills you will see outlined in this book, something miraculous has happened. Even the writing of this book took place because I disciplined myself to focus on contributing a book that would make a difference in the lives of those who read it. The key to your success is to do exactly the same thing—*focus!*

This book is for all of you who wish to achieve some measure of greatness in your life, but have found yourself lacking in self-discipline, disbelieving in your own worth, challenged in the setting and achieving of goals, and losing the right perspective of failing to put people before things.

The first two chapters cover the most important principle of focusing on success, that of *belief.* You'll discover how critical the act of believing is in moving yourself forward. Chapters 3 and 4 build on belief by emphasizing the need for a positive *attitude* as the second principle and skill to develop. Your attitude will determine whether you doubt or believe you will succeed.

Next, comes the setting of *goals* in chapters 5 and 6. Here is where you will learn to really get focused on the life success you want to achieve. These chapters will guide you through one method that has helped me to focus and reach my dreams.

While the whole book is on focusing on success, chapters 7 and 8 give you some concrete examples from my own life on what happens when you lose and regain *focus.* You must stay committed and focused on your dreams. These chapters will definitely help you. Even after I completed writing this book I had to stay super focused to see it through to being printed.

With all the literature on shooting for success it was important for me to stress the need for balance with *relationships* and achievements. So chapters 9 and 10 will assist you in gaining the perspective you need to work on your personal relationships.

Finally, chapters 11 and 12 will help you see how belief without *action* never has enough power to be truly focused in making your success. Action is a key attribute but it cannot come without the previous principles as a foundation to jump from.

All of these areas require you to do something that all successful athletes have learned. It is the skill that accomplished musicians have long mastered. For many self-made millionaires it has been an inherent ability that they have skillfully drawn upon. For the artistic person it is the secret behind their creations on paper or in art form that magically let us see things we have previously ignored. It is the effort that a child in kindergarten puts into writing their name for the very first time.

For each of these successes and all the ones that remain for you to achieve, you must learn to do just one thing. *FOCUS!*

It is my sincere hope that you will try out the art and practice of focusing on success in your own life. Write me and let me know of the success you have achieved by focusing. Maybe your contributions will see themselves in future editions of this book, or in a completely new book.

Whatever your goals and aspirations are, I wish you all the joy and happiness you desire, which is really the ultimate *focus on success.*

Roy Saunderson
London, Ontario, Canada

BELIEVING IN THE MAGIC WITHIN YOU!

Writing this book has been an amazing thing. For a long time I have told myself, and those around me, I was going to write a book. But somehow a voice in the back of my head kept telling me "you don't have time". And, "who do you think you are anyways, writing a book?"

Well, the next thing I had to do was to really believe I could write a book. After all, I have been speaking professionally for over nine years. I have a few magazine articles to my credit. So if I can talk I can write, and if I can write an article I can string a few more together to make a chapter. And if I put a few chapters together...well, you get the picture!

And therein lies the key! You have to get the picture. You have to see what you want to achieve in your mind's eye. Make it so you can smell it, feel it, and see it in you mind in 3-D Technicolor. It must be so vivid you want to reach out and grab it! If you claim you want success badly enough, you have to believe you can do it with every fibre of your body.

You have to desire with a burning fire of passion, to do whatever it's going to take to let go of the negatives, move away from the security blanket of complacency, and do as the famous Nike motto has told us...*just do it!*

A Little Bit About Me

You need to know something about me since we are going to be spending some time together.

I am not an overnight success story. Nor do I see myself as having reached the pinnacle of success even as I speak to you right now (O.K., I'm writing to you!). In every way I am as much a student of success as you are. So in that light I am succeeding in focusing on success. In fact, I believe success is an ongoing journey of one achievement after another. One success builds upon another until you find another goal you wish to reach for.

You can probably tell from my accent (try to imagine, now) that I didn't start out in North America. My life starts out in a town called Great Bookham, Surrey, just south of London, England.

My Dad had a tough start in fatherhood as his dear sweetheart and wife died giving birth to me. He walked the several miles home from the hospital in the early hours of the morning. So began his incredible challenge of rearing an infant alone while grieving, and still going daily to work.

My soon to be godmother looked after me during the daytime until Dad got home from work each night. My earliest memories of my godmother, affectionately called Aunt Cath, were of throwing my stuffed toys into the boiler of a washing machine.

Dad remarried when I was two, and from all accounts I was a typical two-year-old.

School started when I was five years old. I enjoyed the sandbox and the water activity centre. People got worried when I played with the same toy truck all day. Hey, you can do a lot with a toy truck! What was the matter?

The early years of school were uneventful. At least, I don't recall anything, and no-one seemed to be complaining. Then, as elementary school moved along, my tongue and my lack of self-confidence got in the way of good marks. I was always talking in class. Teachers would send me out of the classroom and I would carefully avoid the principal by pretending to go to the washroom, then quickly return outside the classroom door before I was missed.

If only my teachers could see that years later I would get *paid* for talking!

My lack of self-confidence came from being weak in social skills, being repeatedly picked on by the bullies, and being a skinny runt who was always the last one picked for team sports. And so I made up for all of this by seeking everyone's attention as the class clown.

Bottom line was I did not appear to be too smart, and my marks showed it. What I didn't know, is that it was what I *believed* I couldn't do that gave me the C's and D's on my report card. My parents did the best they could to motivate me. While I was lovingly lectured on the merits of a good education, they also tried the comparison technique. I was compared with a Christopher Pelton who lived on a nearby street and *always* got good marks.

You, too, may have found yourself compared with someone in your childhood, whether it was a studious sibling or peer. It doesn't feel good. You find yourself resenting the other person, and they may never know they are being used as a measuring stick. Wherever you are, Chris, I hope your ears aren't burning!

School days seemed to be tough days for me at that point. And my report card was a visible barometer of how I was feeling about myself on the inside.

Branding Of A Label

Then an interesting event occurred. During the 1960s they had a national standardized exam in England called the 11+ (plus) Exam, so called because it was done at eleven years of age. If you passed it, you could move from the regular public school system to the more elite grammar school system.

Those of average intelligence stayed in the regular school system and were streamed into the "A" classes. If you failed miserably, you were relegated to the "B" class. Guess who ended up in the "B" class? Yours truly!

At age 11 I wasn't very happy with myself, or life in general. While I can't recall now, I would not be surprised if my result on the 11+ exam was the explanation.

I did a stupid thing at that time. I don't even know where the idea came from. But I do clearly recall going to my bedroom one day and unscrewing the cover off of the light switch. I put my fingers on the two wires and...*Zapp!!!* I was thrown back on to my bed. Being a glutton for punishment and a slow learner, I tried it again. Same result as before. I got a large jolt of electricity and a free ride towards my bed. Yes, at that young age I was trying to put an end to things.

I don't believe I was thinking suicide. I was just trying to hide from my problems and the knowledge that deep inside I was responsible for what was happening with my school marks.

I am grateful I am still very much alive. I am glad I have gone on to live the experiences that I can now share with you.

The real problem I had back then, was I did not believe in myself.

A New Beginning

Now here is where the beginning of belief starts to happen for me, but I was blind to it in my youth. If only someone had been around who could have helped me focus on *believing,* maybe I would have seen success earlier in my life.

After I did the 11+ test, we moved to another town. This was where my Mom's sister, my aunt, and all my cousins lived. Mom took me to the new school accompanied by my aunt and cousins. We met the principal, known as a head-master in England, and he simply asked my Mom how old I was. She answered the same age as Margaret, my cousin. His immediate reply was to put me in the same class as my cousin. I knew she was in the "A" class, but I wasn't going to tell any-one! (I recently thanked my cousin for this breakthrough in my life, and the number of times I have mentioned her in public).

Now here's the clincher. I did just fine in the "A" stream classes. In other words, I lived up to the new label that was placed upon me. So what happened? All kinds of *believing* things were going on.

The principal believed a good environment to a newcomer would be to place me in the same class as my cousin. The teacher naturally believed the principal that I must be an "A' stream student and treated me as such. Same with my fellow class mates. And me? My academic performance was poor to average. I hadn't learned to *believe* the new label yet.

You may see some similar experiences in your own life where you doubted yourself and lacked self-confidence. Perhaps, like my own example, your early years in life were not as successful as you would have liked them to have been. Can you see how believing in yourself, acknowledging you just might possess some unique potential and abilities, could have helped you soar above whatever challenges you were facing in your childhood?

Each of us comes into this world with great value. We have the potential to grow and blossom or to lie down and be trampled upon. Even within the various life circumstances we find ourselves in, we can learn to rise above them. In this we must choose between mediocrity or greatness.

Finding Something To Focus On

Teenage years are challenging ones. I can look back now and see I was desperately searching for answers to the big questions, about my own identity and the purpose of life. In a small town, and with only a youth's perception of life, I had no idea what success was nor who to ask.

I had discovered the library and ate up the limited collection of books on success, motivation, philosophy, and all religions. I brought home one book without having perused the contents ahead of time. I was caught up with the words "power' and "thinking" and felt this book might give me the ultimate secrets of success.

Then the title of the first chapter took me aback. "Believe In Yourself". Did I? I was always looking for something outside of me to be the solution to all my problems. But believing in myself...this was not easy.

Needless to say, Norman Vincent Peale's book, *The Power of Positive Thinking,* made a lasting impression upon my life. Its principles and suggestions kept me on the right side of life during those critical adolescent years, and they would stay with me right up to the present day.

I eventually wrote Dr. Peale when I entered professional speaking, and thanked him for his book and the difference he had made in my life. In return, he not only wrote me back but sent me one of his latest books, *The Power of Positive Living.* How kind for such a busy and famous person as Dr. Norman Vincent Peale, to keep on giving even when receiving.

So I had found the beginnings of something to focus on, namely, myself. Do you believe in yourself? Do you believe that right now, independent of any performance on your part, you are special and can achieve anything you set your heart and mind on?

This is one of the most important belief principles you must learn to achieve the success you desire.

The Secret to Believing In Yourself

That last question from the previous paragraph (go ahead and read it again) holds the answer to how you can focus on believing in yourself and beginning your journey to success.

Too many times I have seen success measured by school grades and percentages, promotions and athletic records, the length of academic letters after a name, and finally the almighty dollar or whatever currency is applicable to you. These are the external markers by which many in our world today measure success.

Now the question you have to ask yourself is whether you believe that you are a success without these performance indicators. Can you really see in your mind's eye and feel in your soul that you are a very special person, even before you get out of bed or lift a finger to do any task? And the final key to success in that earlier question was whether you could believe those things and achieve anything you set your *heart* and *mind* on.

For a long time I have been filling my *mind* with motivation, success, positive thinking, and behavioural concepts, words and thoughts from the greatest leaders and motivational writers and speakers that you can possibly name. Now I am beginning to see a shift in my life towards greater success than I have ever seen before and it is because of that other word: *heart*.

Follow Your Heart, And You'll Never Go Wrong

After attending a convention of the National Speakers Association in Orlando, Florida and both listening to and personally speaking with motivational speaker, Les Brown, I realized that in order to have "passion" the way Les says it, you have to have it in your heart first.

He shared with us at a benefit seminar how to make an impact on your audience with the stories we tell. Naturally, Les showed us with a powerful story that so captured our emotions, we fell silent. Then he eased the tension with some related humour around the same event in his life. According to Les, the art of making an impact requires you to _live_ the event, to _experience_ it again like you did the first time, so that your audience will _feel_ it with you.

This kind of experience can only be felt with your heart, and the interesting thing is that one way or another, whether it's with watery eyes, actual tears, or just plain attentiveness, you know you are _moved_ by the story.

That's when it hit me! Yes, my ears heard the words which transferred a signal to my brain, which perceived them in the right order for me to understand them according to my own life experience. But it was my heart that _felt_ the emotions, the feelings, the stirrings, that made me want to do something.

And so it is with our focus on success, and the need to focus on belief. We first must hold the belief of what it is we want to achieve, and hold it firmly in our mind. Then we must put the _fire in our belly_ by kindling the passion in our hearts to really move us into action. In this way, our heart becomes the source of the steam to propel us into action. Our mind becomes the track to steer the engine; the boom with its sail to catch the force of the wind gusting from our inner heart of desire; the internal motivation that makes us move in the right direction.

As Les Brown asked his audience in Orlando, Florida, _"what is it that will motivate you to get out of your comfort zone?"_. Is it your faith, family, relationships, success, money, position, fame? Can you make yourself feel that your goal and vision of success is a calling only you can answer? For in reality there is only one person exactly like you in the whole world. You are the only person who can make a difference in the world the way you can. So what is it that will stir your heart into action?

Love What You Do So Much
You'd Do It For Free

The bottom-line regarding your heart is that we attribute the feeling of love coming from our heart. So at sometime or another you are going to have to ask yourself what it is you *love* to do. What is it that gets you all tingly and excited about doing? What do you lie awake at night thinking about? What is one thing that you do well and others tell you so? What do you dream about doing? What is it that you love to do so much, that you would even do it for free just to experience what gives you that sense of satisfaction?

For me, it is speaking to audiences. I want to be able to touch just one heart and make a difference in that person's life. I love the adrenaline charge I experience when an audience and I are so connected that some special, spontaneous moments are shared. And I didn't discover this until I was 31 years of age.

Oh, I was happy in the healthcare profession I was trained in. Very much so, in fact. But when I discovered the whole atmosphere and creativity and excitement of putting together a presentation, and seeing the impact of words and stories on the lives of others... I was hooked!

Why? Because I loved it! I *felt* different, special, yes, even glowing inside when I spoke. There was genuine inspiration as each presentation was crafted. Each practice became a recharging of enthusiasm towards the day of the actual event. And on the day, I can be like a caged animal pacing to be let out and be free to perform. I often have to do some relaxation exercises just to bring me down from the anticipated excitement.

Yes, if you can't tell already, I love to speak!

What is that you presently love to do or wish that you could be doing? All you really need to be successful in life is to discover things you love to do, and then do them.

Whatever Your Heart Desires

It's amazing how our language uses the word heart over and over again. Expressions like, *"Put your whole heart into it"; "I didn't have the heart to tell you"; "My heart aches for you";* and *"Can we have a heart-to-heart discussion"* all show the value we place on the metaphoric meaning of the word "heart".

The heart is the primary muscle of the human body. It pumps the life source of blood carrying oxygen and needed nutrients and discards what the body does not need, like carbon dioxide so the lungs can exhale it and the body is kept clean and pure from these body pollutants.

But what about our focus on belief and achieving success? How can the heart help us here?

To desire something is to long for and hope for something. You can have a strong wish that you may have expressed to someone else, or maybe just to yourself. Many of us hope for success in some area of our lives, whether it is with relationships, health, or financial independence. What will give this wish life, is not to keep on looking for Aladdin's lamp and hope that the genie is still locked inside. No, the life source of power and energy that will propel your wish into living reality is placing your wish in your heart, and seeing it take form one day at a time.

A desire is just a beginning. It is like a seed of an idea. You have to plant it first because the seed may be in your hand, but it will never sprout unless you put it in the right situation for it to germinate. We all know the rest of what happens, as any kindergarten or grade one child can tell you from putting a bean seed in a glass on some paper towel or cotton batting.

Have you seen how a child inspects the glass everyday for even a glimpse of the first sprouting of a root? And thereafter They faithfully visit their new creation every day and give it the water and light it needs.

What seed of an idea do you have that you have been holding in your hand for too long? Interestingly, you are holding my seed in your hand right now. Oh, I know it's no longer in seed form. I hope this living thing of a book gets you as excited about your ideas as the first keypunch on the computer was for me.

As Larry Winget , a professional speaker who inspired me to get going on my book, said, I guess I don't believe much in my topics or my audiences if I don't have books or tapes for them. Now they will remember what I have said and gain some additional ideas on how they can make a difference.

What is it you want to achieve again? For some of you it will be to become self-employed. Others will have formal education in mind and a longing for a specific career. A few of you will aspire to positions of fame. Others are wanting to devote their lives to humanitarian causes. There are budding authors among you, poets, songwriters, artists, and performers extraordinaire.

For a long time I thought I was going to be the next Tom Jones or Engelbert Humperdink and become a professional singer. I pursued this and asked an actor who regularly came into the bank I worked at for the name of a singing teacher. He gave me the name of a teacher who had worked with some of the best in the business, most noted being Paul Anka. I went from being off key to actually being able to sing!

My teacher suggested my stiff upper lip, and body to match, needed some coaching through dancing. So I ended up taking modern jazz and loosened up from my more rigid pose.

By now I was beginning to see myself as a singer. I attended as many concerts as I could. With my new-found confidence and belief in myself, I would ask and arrange to go backstage and personally meet with these celebrities. Always I would ask how they managed to perform the way they did and learn more about their singing technique.

And then came the crunch time. A shortage of money was arising in my life and I felt I had no solution but to discontinue my lessons.

I was 18 years of age. I didn't know then what I now know about a burning desire. And so the dream of being a singer was buried. The flame that was glowing was snuffed out by a world that offered no answer to focusing on belief and pursuing one's dreams.

But as I look back I can see how that *"once-upon-a-time"* desire, that small seed, took root and started to swell up. I did things then as a 17 and 18 year old that most people never dream of doing. In one day I orchestrated a backstage, one-on-one meeting with Vicki Carr and Tony Bennett, to the exclusion of other celebrities wanting to see them. Now I ask myself, why didn't I draw on these experiences to catapult me further along the road of success? You'll discover the answer to this question in the next chapter. You must begin to move your belief into action!

Focus Points On Belief

Point #1: Belief keeps good labels glued on and can get bad labels peeled off. Make time just to believe all the good things about you!

Point #2: Belief starts as an attitude in your mind and must be maintained by the passion of your heart. Put your heart into everything you do.

Point #3: Answer this question I heard from Les Brown: "What is it that would get you to get out of your comfort zone?". Then go do it and get comfortable with it.

Point #4: When you can *feel* the belief and have the answer to getting out of your comfort zone, nothing can stop you from focusing on success.

Point #5: If you don't love what you are doing, isn't it about time you found something you do love?

PUTTING BELIEF INTO ACTION

Why do we not learn from previous experiences? I think I know the answer to that question. It's because we don't see them as being even similar to our present situation. Now this *seeing* is both literal and figurative. Somehow, our wonderful brain has recorded in our mind these experiences but without any connection.

This is where the heart part comes in. When you really *feel* something about a wish or a goal you want to reach, the brain fires up all kinds of chemical juices that create synaptic connections between cells in the brain. This is when creativity sparks! Ideas come flashing to the forefront. Connections between previous thoughts, ideas and actual experiences are somehow brought forward for consideration.

These ideas and thoughts were always there, but without a burning desire to heat them up in the crucible of creativity, they were lying like dead embers from a long winter fire.

Seeing Really Is Believing

Okay. This is going to be the toughest part of belief. You are going to have to stretch yourself like you wouldn't believe. That sounds contradictory since I *do* want you to believe! Anyway, you have a goal of something you want to have or something you want to do or become. In order to achieve this goal you have to see it so clearly in your mind's eye you can reach out and touch it. You have to be living your new position or job so vividly, you can hear yourself talking to people on the job right in your head and see every movement that you and the characters in your mind are doing. Whatever the goal, see it in your mind.

Yes, you have to see it first and then you can believe it. And when you can believe it because you can see it, watch out because things are going to start happening that you could never have counted on.

The Proof Of Believing

Let me share with you an experience from when I was going to graduate school at Wayne State University in Detroit, Michigan, while living in Windsor, Ontario. It was cheaper to live in Canada as we lived in government housing and I still had to pay non-resident tuition fees wherever I was living.

I am now down to my last semester. I had to pay approximately $3,000 Canadian dollars each semester, so we were up to, and beyond, our eyeballs in debt to family and the government with school loans. Yet in this last semester I was $1,000 short. There seemed to be no other sources of money available.

Now you have to know that I had not gotten this far in life–24 years of age at the time, married, and father of three very young children–without having a lot of faith in God. We had been in tight spots before but never quite this tight. When you believe in something so much like completing an education and *seeing* yourself as getting this one particular job in another city as I did, you know you're not going to let something like a "little" bit of money get in the way. You have to see what you want in your own life and never let go of your dream.

My part-time job was not offering any more hours. I had a few options left. I could go to school part-time and find another part-time job. The downside would be losing out on the job I wanted after I got my degree. I could work full-time for awhile and save the money I needed. Or I could register, take the courses, and hope that something would work out.

Many of my friends told me I had come too far to bail out or lose the job I wanted in London, Ontario. The feelings (there's that *feeling* from the heart again!) I had were to register. Somehow everything would work itself out.

Taking A Leap Of Faith

An interesting thing happens when you take a risk, stretch that old comfort zone, and do something that doesn't quite make sense...like registering when you know you don't have any money. From a spiritual perspective, I knew of many examples from the scriptures, as well as personal experiences, of individuals who took a leap of faith only to be blessed with what they needed.

My wife and I laughed as I went ahead and registered. It would not be the last time we would laugh at leaping with faith, as I'll share with you later. We knew that job in the city of London was for me. We could *see* that, hard though that was to explain to those around us. But I think some of you will understand what I mean from similar experiences you have had too.

Then, as if real light bulbs went on above my head, I had a brilliant idea that I know came from an inspired source because it wasn't there before. For me, this was an answer to prayer.

Since I was training to be a speech-language pathologist I agreed in my mind to forfeit the job I wanted in London in exchange for any health care organization loaning me the money I needed of $1,000. In return, I would sign a contract agreeing to work for them for a minimum of two years and the borrowed money would be deducted out of my salary.

It seemed like a pretty good idea to me. In fact, every organization I called told me how impressed they were with my ingenuity in coming up with such an idea. Only problem was, they wouldn't give me any money!

Faith Has To Precede The Miracle

Now whether you believe in God, as I do, or some Higher Power or powers of the universe, everything I've told you about *believing*, *feeling* in your heart, *seeing* things in your mind, and *desiring* what you want, reaches out to others who in turn reach out to you.

And that's exactly what happened to us on this occasion. Far away in Washington, DC, my wife's parents were doing volunteer work for our church. They had another older lady sharing the apartment with them. We had not bothered my wife's parents on this latest financial episode since they had helped us out before.

It so happened that my wife's parents were coming to visit us for a couple of weeks. This other lady said to them that she *felt* (you've got to listen to those promptings!) as if she knew us through our letters to them. She said she wanted to write us a letter and send us a "little" something.

Well, we met our parents at the border and then they mentioned that they had this letter from their friend for us. It wished us well, hoped all was going all right with my studies, and then concluded with *"I felt impressed to send the enclosed cheque."* The cheque remained in the opened envelope. I pulled it out. Lo, and behold, I was now holding a cheque made out in our names in the amount of ..... $1,000!

What I learned from this experience was that you have to go beyond just believing, feeling, seeing and desiring. There is one more thing that you have to do. You have to get up from where you are sitting and *do something.* Or in my case for writing this book, I actually had to sit down and put fingers to the keyboard.

And then there is that wonderful Law of the Harvest of whatever you sow you will one day reap. If you don't ever sow that seed of an idea and nurture and work at it, it will never happen. But when you work and toil at an idea you are so *passionate* about, something is going to have to give in the universe and make room for what you need.

We will always be indebted to our benefactor from Washington and the divine powers that brought this miracle to pass in our lives at that time. It would be the foundation of faith for further miracles.

Focus on Action

You can focus on believing until you're blue in the face and your belly button has collected a ton of lint! But until you step out and do something, nothing else is going to change. I had to do a lot of homework to find out the possible organizations to approach for money. It was not exactly easy or enjoyable to make those phone calls, I can tell you, but they got easier once I got going.

That fact reveals an interesting truth about action. The more actions you do towards your desired outcome, the easier it becomes to do another action, no matter how different or completely disassociated it is from the first action.

Anytime I've become stuck in my life, bogged down in what I believe in but which isn't happening, or seeing a vision of an idea that could make a huge difference, the solution has always been *"what one action do I need to be doing right now?"*. It is not a lot of actions all at once. Uh-uh! All it takes in just one eentsy, weentsy step and feeling the exhilaration of breaking the comfort barrier. Notice, also, that it is *right now* and not later on. And you just keep asking the same question and completing the answer, and most importantly *doing* whatever the answer is. It's that simple, but millions fight it.

What is the one thing you need to be doing right now to help make you a success? Reflect on that for just one minute with your eyes closed.

Take time out now for one minute and close your eyes and reflect on what you should do to achieve a success you desire.

What did you *see* or *feel* you should be doing? Do yourself a favour and put this book down and go and do whatever it was you *felt* impressed to do. Go on ! I can wait for you.

Now, that was pretty easy and I am sure it felt good. I hope you are not cheating and reading ahead. Only those who really stopped and acted upon that impression will find the greatest benefit out of the next chapter.

Those who didn't stop to do what they know they should have done, will find out *why* they didn't in the next chapter as well.

But before we move on to the next focus area, there is one more key to making the principle of belief an important part of your life.

Living Your Dream

I don't know about you, but I hardly ever remember my dreams. If I awaken in the middle of a dream, I can tell you vividly what happened but you had better ask me right away or it will disappear into mid air.

This past summer as we drove through Atlanta, Georgia on the day of the opening ceremonies of the 1996 Olympic Games, you could feel the electricity of excitement as this incredible city prepared to welcome the world's greatest athletes into their midst.

For four years and more, these athletes had prepared to come to hot, humid Atlanta to fulfill a life-long dream. For some it was to have actually made it to the Olympics. Others were moved by patriotic honour to represent their country. Some knew they would never earn a medal but came to achieve their personal best and nothing more. And then there were those few who individually, or collectively as a team, retold the dream of winning a medal and surpassing their most recent personal best.

Our destination was not Atlanta. But before driving on to Orlando, Florida we stopped for some souvenirs.

Besides buying pictures of Olympic sites on postcards, my wife also picked up a postcard of the gravesite of Dr. Martin Luther King, Jr.. On the postcard it had those immortal words of Dr. King that all of us have heard at some point in our lives, of   *"I have a dream..."*. Let me quote the words on the postcard for you:

> *"I have a dream...that one day on the red hills of Georgia, sons of former slaves and sons of former slave-owners will be able to sit down together at the table of brotherhood. I have a dream my four little children will one day live in a nation where they will not be judged by the color of their skin but by the content of their character. I have a dream today!"*

I hope you can see this great man's dream in your mind. And how fitting to have the Olympic Games with the "brotherhood" of the world at one "table" in the Atlanta Olympic Stadium. Martin Luther King, Jr. held tremendous *passion* for his dream. It was his life's purpose to fulfill that dream. And each one of us must have our own dream that may have to outlive us as well. It must be a personal focus that is bigger than any of us. It must be centered on making the world a better place and at no personal gain to ourselves.

Living Life To The Fullest

Yes! In order for you to be truly successful you must live your life everyday as if it were your last. If you were to dream your last dream in your mortal life, I believe there would not be one dream that would not contain people in it. You would see those who you hold dear to your heart and love and cherish. You would recall the incredible, fun-filled memories and experiences with family and friends. For after all is said and done, it is not the material achievements that make us happy and successful. It is *relationships* and the mark for good that we have left upon this planet and the people we have touched.

And so as you develop a firmer belief in yourself and the success that you want to achieve, ask yourself what life purpose you will have that will be your *"I have a dream"* passion. Once you have this "dream" deeply imbedded in your heart and mind, there is nothing that can stop you from achieving your purpose, or having your life purpose continuing beyond your own life.

Discovering Your Real Self

One of the reasons I did not discover my "dream" for reaching success, was because of the labels of the past that I had allowed to hold me back like a ball and chain, never to be removed. These were the labels of *"you'll never amount to much"; "you can't do that"; "you are a 'C' student"; "we don't want him on our team!";* all of the put downs we get thrown at us. And while these words were probably not given with the intent to hurt, you and I know they take their toll.

But here is the simple solution. Focus on today and not the past! Focus on fixing the problem and not the blame.

For me this took the form of some counseling. I borrowed some money to take an executive development program because I could see myself repeatedly wanting to run away from conflict at work and go find another job as the solution.

Like many interpersonal conflicts this was a self-esteem issue I was facing.

Through the executive development program I received a full psychological assessment, a job attribute survey and a counseling interview. At the age of 20 I guess I revealed more than the average executive would about themselves. Then came the results.

Seems I had a habit of blaming everyone else but me for the situation I was in and the problems I encountered. When the psychologist and the counselor assigned to me met to discuss the results, I felt as if I had been clobbered over the head with a huge two by four piece of wood. They told me that I was the one responsible for the belief I had of myself. No matter where the influence of the past came from, I now had total responsibility for believing whatever I wanted to choose about my worth and potential.

That night as I rode the Toronto subway home from my session, the combination of rhythmic to and fro of the train and my mind flooded with thoughts, created a hypnotic picture. While I acknowledged that for years I had been blaming other people for my circumstances, it seemed as if I was now watching a movie of my life with myself stark naked, and I was the lead character in all my life's events. I was the one responsible for my life.

With my counselor helping me to see my assets in life and gradually working on my liabilities, I completed the program in record time. I was able to resolve my work conflicts. I had found the *belief* in myself to do things I had never thought possible.

While not all of us need counseling, I include this experience to demonstrate that there is nothing wrong in seeking professional help, particularly if you have severe low self-esteem.

It is critical that you discover the magic of believing in yourself before you can ever venture forth to achieve any lasting success.

So how do you keep this focus on belief and not lose it? This is where you have to draw on the incredible powers of Attitude, which is the focus of our next chapter.

Focus Points On Belief

Point #1: You have to *feel* passion. If you're not feeling passion towards your focus of success, you will never do what is necessary to reach your dream. Feel the passion.

Point #2: Define very clearly what it is you want to achieve as your focus for success and write it down on paper.

Point #3: Look at your past successes. Each one required that you come to the cliff and jump. Discover and re-live what helped you to jump. Now, replicate that magic, come to the cliff, and this time fly!

Point #4: Add confidence to your belief with action. Do something, no matter how small, each day for your focus on success. The secret of action is to begin.

Point #5: If you have a dream live it. Never let anyone destroy your dream. It's yours, and its beautiful. Sleep on it!

FOCUSING ON ATTITUDE

It's a shame that over the last few years the common vernacular has given the word "attitude" a negative connotation. Really, it's quite a neutral word and means simply "to have a mental position or feeling regarding something". This can naturally be either positive or negative, but one way or another you *do* have an attitude.

Now this is encouraging to know that each of us has an attitude. All we have to do is make sure that we have the right mental position or feeling regarding the success we want to achieve.

Easier said than done, right? I know what you mean. I have been my own worst enemy, which is always the case with attitude. You are in control of the direction your attitude is taking. You can change the direction at any time by simply thinking positive or negative thoughts. Your attitude will become even more permanent in the position it holds by the actions you take. That's why I'm telling you that you have to do one thing today, no matter how small it is, towards whatever goal or dream you want to accomplish.

I'm as human as the rest of you, and I have shot myself in the attitudinal foot many times. If you don't think I didn't get discouraged when those healthcare organizations didn't pan out with the $1,000 I needed, you're mistaken!

I had to "attitudinize" myself. Sure, go look the word up in the dictionary, I didn't make it up. It means to assume an affected mental attitude. In my mind that means to take on a positive, optimistic outlook on the matter at hand. That for me is an "affected mental attitude".

The reverse of this is an "*in*fected mental attitude". You know, the negative put downs and self-talk of what we can't do and our long list of reasons for why we can never do what we claim we want to achieve. It's the pessimist that we allow into our heads. And just as I described it, it will infect your whole body and being. It will sap the strength right out of you as good as any physical infection can.

You cannot allow this infection to remain untreated for long or you will lose your belief in the success you want to achieve.

Beyond A Shadow Of A Doubt

In the chapter on focusing on belief, I shared with you how desire starts off really small and sows its seed of hope towards an idea you have in your mind. In exactly the same way, doubt starts off as a negative vine winding its way through the thoughts of your brain until it has strangled or sucked out all life from your beginning seed that was growing.

In our own childhood we ventured off to do something that we could see ourselves doing. Meanwhile, always behind us, was a childhood enemy, sometimes a parent, or even a teacher who said those haunting words: "I doubt you can do that!". Depending how fragile our self-esteem was, those words could hinder our performance, or at worst stop us all together. For some people who have fed their minds repeatedly with positive attitudes about who they really are and what they can do, such phrases can be just the catalyst to prove others wrong!

There have been many times in my life I have doubted my own abilities. I have halted my own progress based on the opinions of others. On occasion I have let these doubts take on a life of their own, where they appeared so real they must be true. Or were they?

Somewhere in my mind where my own desires and wishes had begun, there was hope, a longed for belief to do something that I wanted. You have those same feelings too! You have to focus on them. You can't ever stop focusing on what you want to achieve. You have to see it in those wonderful glasses of hope. You may have to use a telescope because your goal seems such a long ways away. But focus, focus, focus!

Never lose sight of your goal!

Do The Thing You Fear!

If you let doubt take a rest in your mind too long, it will grow into a redwood of a tree called "fear"! Californian redwoods are those thousands of years old trees that the tourist magazines show cars driving through, that's how thick they are. And fear can become equally as thick and tall but you won't be able to drive through it unless you remove the beginning doubts in the first place.

Motivational speaker, Zig Ziglar, has a wonderful definition of fear using the word itself as an acronym. He says fear is *False Evidence Appearing Real.* I like his interpretation.

Think about the things you have feared in your life. For me I am still not a confident swimmer and have never taken swimming lessons. I have this belief stuck in my head that I cannot float. So my "false evidence" is that all things in water sink, including me! Now it does "appear real" to me every time I lose control. But the fact is, I have never drowned or you wouldn't be reading this book!

Rising To New Heights

But one of my greatest fears was heights.

I was always scared when I went out with friends and they wanted to climb to the top of the tallest tree in the woods. Somehow I made it at least halfway up, always looking down in case I would miss a branch and fall.

Then I met Adrian. We must have been around 11 years of age. We played all the time together.

Adrian wasn't scared of anything. He climbed trees and walls and anything that had a chance to be climbed. Now if I wanted to play with Adrian I had to do the things Adrian did.

Then I did something that holds a lot of weight for solving the fear problems you and I face today. I told Adrian of my fear of heights. Tell someone you trust and respect about your fear. The act of telling gets it out of your head and diminishes the size of the fear.

Well Adrian was a cool kid, and he had the street smarts to know the psychology of a solution. The fear behind heights is falling. So he had me go to a 12 foot high wall that went along a walkway to a parking lot. Without telling me, his innate sense was to teach me to overcome my fear of falling.

First, I had to squeeze under a door to get to the inside of the wall. Then by placing my legs and arms between two walls about 4 feet apart, I had to push with all my strength and climb up this wall. Finally, I was on top of the wall.

Now this wall had a deceiving image that people walking along the pathway never knew. For them the wall was always 12 feet high. From my new vantage point up top, I saw this wall gradually descend on my right hand side to about 30 to 50 feet to the entrance of an underground parking lot.

My friend was like a monkey and he would run along this wall like it was a 10 foot wide pathway. Yours truly, walked very slowly along and was grateful to come to the end so I could jump down.

So we practiced this every Saturday. And slowly but surely I went from walking slowly to going quickly. In time I was able to climb up that wall and run along it at the same speed and manner as my friend.

You can see the secret to overcoming my fear, can't you? It was simply to do what I feared until the feelings of fear disappeared.

What do you fear? Do you feel you do not have the experience to do well what you want to do? Then learn from others and practice, practice, practice! Ask for help from others. Interview people who do what you want to do and apply what they tell you. Seek out a mentor who is prepared to guide you.

Do you fear that you are too old to start over? Remember Colonel Sanders started Kentucky Fried Chicken financed with his Old Age Security cheque. The Delaney sisters had a writer help them write down their thoughts and experiences of growing up as African-Americans and they're both over 100 years of age and now have two books to their credit. And just the other day I was flipping the radio stations and heard of Jeanne Calment in France, who at 121 years of age, and purported to be the oldest living woman, had just made a rap CD entitled *Mistress of Time*! Now beat that!

So you have to do what Susan Jeffers says, which became the title of her successful book, that is "feel the fear and do it anyways".

Making The Unknown A Friend

Some degree of fear is understandable and is actually a physical body response to the unknown. Take for example a roller-coaster ride. You stay in line for hours to get on. The closer you get to the front of the line the quieter you get or the more hyper you become and you can't shut up. Then you're on board and usually with a friend to share the experience. The ride takes you through some twists and turns, up and down, swings you at high speeds, gives you some false expectations leading to the most terrifying drop of the ride. You eventually get off the ride with a sense of relief and accomplishment, and you exclaim to everyone's amazement, "let's go do it again!"

You may ask what's wrong with this picture but we've either seen it or experienced it. We mislabeled the feelings that our body was experiencing. The body has its own defense mechanism for when danger lurks and releases chemicals like adrenaline that prepare us to fight or flee the unknown. In the roller coaster example, we had no idea what to expect. Once you had actually experienced it for yourself you were able to label the ride as a positive adrenaline surge and not a negative fear.

Many people have the same negative expectation towards public speaking. You've all heard the *Book of Lists* statistic that claims people would rather die than give a speech. The joke that goes with this is that people would rather be in the coffin than giving the eulogy. What is fearful for some is my personal natural high. I love being a professional speaker and delivering a message that will impact people's lives through keynote presentations or provide concrete practical skills in a seminar.

Your way to face the unknown is to do just that, face the unknown. Face it head on. Ask yourself what would be the worst thing that could happen to you. This idea of negative preparation allows you to be prepared for anything in advance. Now you can strategize a solution.

Creating The Courage To Risk

For a long time I had held back launching my own business full-time. It was easier to do it part-time and maintain the security of a full-time job. Until the harsh reality hit of no longer having a full-time job to hang onto. The so-called security was purely a perception held by myself and many others. All of us are at the mercy of supply and demand and the economic pressures of a changing global market place.

What was for so long considered a great risk is now right on my doorstep and I now enjoy self-employment. It brings me a great deal of control to make my own income and balance my life accordingly. You'll find me banging away at the keyboard at all hours of the day and night creating a book, a letter, or some business development for a client. I can be as creative as I want when I want to be. You bet it's hard work. There is a lot of self-discipline. I'm having to learn a lot of business skills as well.

One of the fears I have had for many years was the fear of success. Every time I had written down goals, I would hear the haunting voices of the past telling me I would never amount to much. When I wrote down goals of wanting financial independence, I realized I was limiting myself by the value of needing to be secure. I would never venture out to try anything.

What I learned from books like Anthony Robbins' *Awaken The Giant Within*, was to change the underlying values that would take me away from achieving my goals. In other words, you and I can end up with some mixed up values that actually hold us back from success.

For me, I realized that I needed the same thing as the cowardly lion in the movie *Wizard of Oz*. Yes, I needed to have courage to go out and risk. Even now I have to pump myself up with the courage to do the things I feel I can't do. Once you have conquered just one of these fears you have earned the right to wear the badge of courage.

So muster up the courage you need right now and step out of your comfort zone. Take hold of the challenge in front of you. Do just one thing today towards accomplishing your dreams and you'll see your fears slip away from you.

Becoming An Attitude Builder

So how can we build the right attitude, that positive perspective and feeling towards success?

The first thing is to reach back to the beliefs you hold about yourself. Do you see yourself as an inherently good person of infinite worth, independent of any skills, talents and attributes? If you do not, then there is a lot of building repairs ahead. If you can see this image, you are already ahead of many people.

You have read a little about how my life began. In my early working years I was always trying to prove myself to others. Yet at the same time I was trying hard to undo the negative statements I allowed myself to repeat inside my head. This created tension and led to headaches associated with stress. When the doctor prescribed valium I made up mind that I was not going to take medication. I was going to figure this out.

Amazingly, I was able to change my job in a short period of time, motivated, no doubt, by my determined attitude. Then I enrolled in an executive development program where I had to borrow a couple of thousand dollars just to pay for it. This program would have me assessed by a psychologist and then I would work with a counselor to find out my ideal career and then be assisted in getting it.

It was a scary day when I heard the psychologist and the counselor describe me to a tee, all based on the testing they had done. With my list of asset and liability qualities, the goal was to get as many of the liabilities removed as possible.

I had a hard time with negative thoughts about myself and others. In order to unlearn this habit I learned the "buzz" technique.

When I had a negative thought, I would have to say "buzz' out loud and then correct that thought with a positive replacement. By actually having the courage to say the word out loud, it was amazing how quickly I was motivated to stop thinking negatively. Now, just imagine doing that at the office or wherever you work! These days I tell myself "stop!" and then I self-correct.

The mind is an interesting place. Once you get rid of a negative thought, you must fill the vacuum made in the mind by its removal with a positive attitude of thoughts, words and images. Even playing uplifting, relaxing music can tune the mind into a rhythmic balance that is peaceful.

Learn to appreciate the beauties of nature around you. Practice relaxation exercises to calm the muscles and hold peaceful images in your mind.

Be careful what you watch on TV, or your VCR, or even at the cinema. Research continues to show that the mind cannot distinguish the difference between that which is visually perceived and that which is vividly imagined. There are too many shows and movies that are negative with violence, sex, and negative language. These thoughts can never be erased. The only thing we can do is to continually "play" a more positive image in our mind in order to block out the negative.

At the same time there are lots of positive and motivational programs or videos you can watch, as well as audiotapes from speakers and authors. And of course reading books will assist you in learning how to maintain the attitude of success.

The bottom-line here is if you have a negative train of thought, don't get on board!

Watch Your Language!

It is becoming increasingly important to not only watch the thoughts we let into our minds, but to take control of the words and language we let out of our mouths. We can create a negative mindset by what we speak as well as by what we see and hear.

Notice how the world around us seems to look at life from a negative viewpoint. The newspapers create huge headlines, and front page priority to what often amounts to be nothing more than trash. And yet to find the story of a valiant act of courage or kindness, you have to hunt for the small headline and column on the back page of the third or fourth section of the paper.

Taking a further look at a topic all of us are well versed at initiating with friend or stranger, even the weather has a negative slant in any report from your local meteorologist. Instead of saying there is 90% chance of sun, they turn it around and tell us how there is a 10% chance of precipitation. You and I have to make a difference where we live and get people overjoyed and excited about 90% chance of sun, hope and success!

I remember hearing motivational speaker Dan Clark share a negative comment he heard in a place you definitely don't want to hear one. He told his audience of the many trips by airplane he has to make in his business. Often you hear the voice of the pilot mention greetings, altitude, and arrival times. But Dan says he sure doesn't like to hear the captain advise the passengers, "We're coming in for our *final descent!*". You certainly hope it isn't your final descent.

Like the pilot who is in control of the altitude of the plane, you are in the pilot seat for controlling the altitude of your attitude.

This will have a huge impact on achieving goals when you get to that chapter. For how you *think* you will do in achieving your goals will determine what you *will* do with those goals.

So if you are concerned about your thinking, then take a good look at your language. Do you use negative words or phrases that show a lack of positive energy? Are you failing to take advantage of the many positive things you could be saying?

Take a look at the following words and ask yourself, how do I feel after only reading these words? How would I react to someone who used these words all the time?

I think	I might
I'll try	Maybe
Perhaps	I hope so
Possibly	I don't know
Sometimes	Pretty good

Don't you sense a total lack of commitment or power in these words?

Now look at the power behind the use of positive words and phrases in the following list. Feel the upbeat, optimistic and energizing effect of these words.

I will	Fantastic!
I can	Great!
I know	Always
Definitely	Absolutely

Imagine you have an unexpected interview in two days. This still gives you a chance to get your suit or dress dry cleaned and returned in time, if it is dropped off before they close today. How would you feel if you gave your suit or dress to your brother and asked if he could run it over to the cleaners for you, and his reply was "I'll try". Would you feel full of confidence that you would have your clothes back in time? I doubt it.

Contrast that with the affirmative reply of *"I will"*. It makes a difference in how you believe, how you look at the world, and in the positive actions you will take towards success, just by what you say.

I find myself challenging people who reply with "pretty good" when I greet them with the question "how are you doing?". Many will look startled at the challenge but can often force themselves to say *"good"* or *"great"*.

So would you please commit to cleaning up your language? This not only means getting rid of profanity because your vocabulary is far richer than that kind of coarse.

Clean out the negatives as well. Answer those questioning greetings of *"How are you?"* with *"great!"* and *"fantastic!"*. Boldly tell people you *will* do what they asked you to do. Speak the positive language of success as a way to focus on your attitude.

Focus Points On Attitude

Point #1: Develop a *"real"* attitude and keep it positive and always alive.

Point #2: When you get an infected mental attitude of the negatives, take at least five positive affirmation antibiotics three times a day. Refills are free so take them as long as you are alive and as needed.

Point #3: Whenever you have a negative train of thought, don't get on board.

Point #4: Fears are not real and are literally a creation of our own thinking. So do the thing you fear just once and find this fact out for yourself.

Point #5: Practice replacing every negative thought and word in your mind, with a beautiful, positive alternative. Make it fun and you will see how quickly you can unlearn negative language.

BUILDING YOUR ATTITUDE

I attended a training program on *Creative Training Techniques* developed by renowned trainer and speaker Bob Pike. Pike pointed out that at some point or another your mind is going to wander. When those moments occur and you get asked a question, he taught us you should jump to attention real quick, and tell the instructor you were *"gone fishing"*.

These wandering moments happen because we think anywhere from 3 to 5 times the rate that we speak. So no wonder when someone is talking to us, we manage to think about a hundred and one things if we're not giving our undivided attention. No wonder we often "go fishing" in our own pond of ideas and imagination.

In the same manner our mind will follow the direction you give it, whether it is positive or negative.

A simple experiment that I do with some of my seminar participants is to show one half of the room the following set of words: orange, apple, peach, banana. The other half of the audience is shown this next set of words: sex, crime, pornography, filth. For the conclusion, I show everyone the following word "R_PE". I ask the first group to shout out the missing letter, and almost to the person they shout back the letter "I". The second group is given the same opportunity, and while a little puzzled, they shout back their response of the letter "A".

Some simple words that were neutral induced the first group to think of a neutral word, while the second group had obviously more emotionally loaded words which induced its response of a more negative word.

This follows the long held computer principle of GIGO, or "garbage in, garbage out". You put bad things into the mind and it will spit back negative thoughts. On the other hand, you feed the mind with positive, uplifting words and thoughts and you can't help but be positive and optimistic about life.

Inspirational quotes, stories, poems, uplifting music, awesome scenes, and powerful imagery, can all have an incredible value and impact in directing the mind on a destination towards success.

Even as I sit at my desk writing this book I see some quotes that lift me up, like:

Goals: No one can predict to what heights you can soar. Even you will not know until you spread your wings.

The scenery for this quote is the silhouette of an eagle with its huge wings spanning a desert sky with the sun shining in the background.

A quote that my oldest daughter handwrote for me on Christmas, states simply: *"Appreciate the assets you already have"*.

A badge that is pinned to a first grade project of a huge pencil holder with the "To Dad" tag still stuck to the can, says:

Who I am makes a difference.

And staring me in the face on a ceramic plaque is Tom Wilson's Ziggy and his dog with the proclamation of *"Have A Rainbow Day"* under a four-coloured version of a rainbow.

To the left of me on my wall is a poem I received from Brian Tracy after I had written him a thank you for the break-through ideas he had shared at a seminar that helped my wife and I focus on getting our first house with no money (I'll share more of that in the chapters on Goals). The poem may be familiar to you. It's entitled "Don't Quit".

"Don't Quit"

When things go wrong as they sometimes will.
When the road you're trudging seems all up hill.
When funds are low and the debts are high.
And you want to smile, but you have to sigh.
When care is pressing you down a bit.
Rest, if you must, but don't you quit.
Life is queer with its twists and turns.
As everyone of us sometimes learns.
And many a failure turns about
When he might have won had he stuck it out:
Don't give up though the pace seems slow --
You may succeed with another blow.
Success is failure turned inside out --
The silver tint of the clouds of doubt.
And you never can tell how close you are.
It may be near when it seems so far:
So stick to the fight when you're hardest hit --
It's when things seem worst that you must not QUIT.

Author Unknown

And finally, the quote that helped me make the decision to leave full-time employment in health care after receiving my lay-off notice from my management position:
You'll always miss 100% of the shots you don't take!

Can you see how quotes and poems like these could put your mind in the right direction?

To help you out in your own collection of inspiring, motivational quotes I have compiled 52 quotes that mean a lot to me personally. You could write them up and cover your walls and mirrors at home or work with them. I have done 52 so you could put a different one up every week. Or you could do as my oldest daughter does and put 26 mini-poster quotes all over her bedroom door.

And if you would like your own *"mini-poster success collection"* of 52 quotes check the back of the book for ordering information.

Don't hesitate to send me your favourite motivational quotes as well. The address to send them to is at the back of the book. I might be able to use them in future books or posters.

So here are the quotations to help you build your attitude.

If one advances confidently in the direction of his dreams and endeavors to live the life which he has imagined, he will meet with a success unexpected in common hours
- Henry David Thoreau

Nothing in the world can take the place of persistence. Talent will not; nothing is more common than unsuccessful men with talent. Genius will not; unrewarded genius is almost a proverb. Education will not; the world is full of educated derelicts. Persistence and determination alone are omnipotent.
- Calvin Coolidge

The 10 most powerful two-letter words are:

If it is to be, it is up to me.

God grant me the serenity to accept the things I cannot change, the courage to change the things I can, and the wisdom to know the difference.

There is little difference in people, but that little difference makes a big difference. The little difference is attitude. The big difference is whether it is positive or negative.

- W. Clement Stone

It is easy in the world to live after the world's opinion; it is easy in solitude to live after our own; but the great man is he who in the midst of the crowd keeps with perfect sweetness the independence of solitude.

- Ralph Waldo Emerson

Never despair. But if you do, work on in despair.

- Edmund Burke

The only certain measure of success is to render more and better service than is expected of you.

- Og Mandino

Set goals and follow through on them. You transform yourself from one of life's spectators into a real participant.

-    Lou Holtz

Nothing will ever be attempted if all possible objections must be first overcome.

- Samuel Johnson

The time is always right to do what is right.
- Martin Luther King, Jr.

Growth means change and change involves risks, stepping from the known to the unknown.
- George Shinn

I'll never forget where I came from and how I got here. Besides, looking back on my own life, I'd say that the secret is not to be without anger but to focus it and generate creative energy from it.
- Robert Guillaume

A new idea is first condemned as ridiculous, and then dismissed as trivial, until finally it becomes what everybody knows.
- William James

To give life a meaning one must have a purpose larger than oneself.
- Will Durant

Most of us dread finding out when we come to die that we have never really lived.
- Henry David Thoreau

What we need is more people who specialize in the impossible.
- Theodore Roethke

Some people see things as they are and ask why. I dream of things that never were and ask why not.

- Robert F. Kennedy

It is our duty as men and women to proceed as though the limits of our ambitions do not exist.

- Pierre Teilhard de Chardin

The greatest pleasure in life is doing what people say you cannot do.

- Walter Bagehot

If you believe in your dreams, there's no limit to what you can do.

- Sam Walton

The best way out is always through.

- Robert Frost

Got troubles and crashing disappointments? Radical change? Dream a new dream! God has provided rich options.

- James Quayle Cannon

I am only one; but still, I am one. I cannot do everything, but still I can do something; I will not refuse to do the something I can do.

- Helen Keller

Just remember, once you're over the hill you begin to pick up speed.

             - Charles Schultz

Kind words can be short and easy to speak, but their echoes are truly endless.

             - Mother Teresa

I don't know the key to success; but the key to failure is trying to please everybody.

             - Bill Cosby

The greatest good you can do for another is not just to share your riches, but to reveal to him his own.

             - Benjamin Disraeli

I push in just one direction, not in every direction.

             - Rita Levi-Montalcini

Don't be afraid to take a big step...you can't cross a chasm in...small jumps.

             - David Lloyd George

In the pursuit of values we discover that life is within, not outside us.

             - Lowell L. Bennion

Remember, luck is opportunity meeting up with preparation, so you must prepare yourself to be lucky.

             - Gregory Hines

What lies behind us and what lies before us are tiny matters compared with what lies within us.

             - Ralph Waldo Emerson

The most delightful surprise in life is to suddenly recognize your own worth.

             - Maxwell Maltz

My interest is in the future because I am going to spend the rest of my life there.

             - Charles F. Kettering

A man is a success if he gets up in the morning and gets to bed at night and in between does what he wants to do.

             - Bob Dylan

I don't know what your destiny will be, but one thing I know: The only ones among you who will be truly happy are those who will have sought and found how to serve.

             - Albert Schweitzer

Do it big, do it right and do it with style.

             - Fred Astaire

The best way to predict the future is to create it.

             - Peter Drucker

I guess the essence of life for me is finding something you enjoy doing that gives meaning to life and then being in a situation where you can do it.

- Isaac Asimov

We cannot become what we need to be by remaining what we are.

- Max DePree

Your work is to discover your work, and then with all your heart to give yourself to it.

- Buddha

We all need to believe in what we are doing.

- Allan D. Gilmour

If you can dream it you can do it.

- Walt Disney

Effort only releases its reward after a person refuses to quit.

- Napoleon Hill

I love my work so much it doesn't seem like work.

- Terry Van Der Tuuk

It is a funny thing about life; if you refuse to accept anything but the best, you very often get it.

- W. Somerset Maugham

Money never starts an idea; it is the idea that starts the money.
                                            - W.J. Cameron

In helping others to succeed we insure our own success.
                                            - William Feather

Always bear in mind that your own resolution to succeed is more important than any one thing.
                                            - Abraham Lincoln

The power of love and caring can change the world.
                                            - James Autry

As you read or scanned each of these truly uplifting quotations, I hope you were *moved* inside to think and feel differently about your life. If you are like me, you will find several of these inspiring phrases will help you know *how to focus on success.*

Write these quotes out; memorize them; read them each day. By focusing on your attitude you will see behaviours you need to work on. As you change those actions and behaviours that need working on, the amazing thing is that your attitude will change to.

Whatever you are focusing your success on, remember to share the wealth with others. Lift others around you with positive expressions and actions. Remember you *can* make a difference. A positive attitude can become contagious. It may seem like a little thing. But it's a big difference if your goal is to focus on something you want to succeed in.

Focus Points On Attitude

Point #1: While driving my children to school, I saw this on a mother's sweatshirt: *"It starts with the right attitude"*. So start your day off right with meditation, affirmations and prayer. By starting right you'll end right.

Point #2: Discover your own feelings as you read inspiring quotations. Ask yourself how those same feelings can help you right now to move into action.

Point #3: Collect your own personal set of quotations that mean a great deal to you. Hopefully, my choices will help you. There is nothing like a line that stirs your soul to help you even more.

Point #4: Put your quotations on full display in your home. My wife started putting the poster set of quotations in a stand in the kitchen and the children automatically read them out loud. Put the power of quotations to full use!

Point #5: Just before you go to bed, read some of your quotes. You will guarantee pleasant dreams and sleep, and a bounty of ideas towards your success when you wake up.

STAYING FOCUSED

Just visit any bookstore and check out the business section. In some form or another you will find the titles have a recurring theme. They are all telling the business person of today to do one thing. Focus!

Whether it is focus on what your purpose and mission is, focus on the customer, or focusing on you, we all need to focus.

Why is this you may ask? Well, I can answer that question from firsthand personal experience and observation of others.

We can all have a dickens of a time focusing on what we know we *should* be doing. And I now know and understand the root cause of the problem. Maybe you are challenged by the same problem I have faced.

You know you want to achieve a particular goal. This means everything in the world to you. You tell everyone about it. Then you start to work on your goal. You have to start with, say, a phone call. You pick up the receiver. Panic starts to set in. You put it back down again. Or else you get through to the right person and now you don't know what to say. You're only glad you didn't leave your name and you hope that the business line doesn't have "call display".

This "fear"—remember, *false evidence appearing real*—may have held you back in the past from making those phone calls. But you have to stop and re-focus on what it is you believe in about yourself. You have to ask myself, "why am I in the profession I've chosen, and what really is the purpose of my business?". As you focus on your business and life purpose, you will start to calm down.

Once you are in a calmer state of mind you can more easily ask yourself the questions that help you solve your panic problem. For example, in the phone call dilemma described above, ask yourself "why?". This will really help. Ask yourself, "why was I scared to make the calls?" Well, you may answer "I didn't know what I was going to say". "So, why didn't you know what you were going to say?". "I guess I hadn't made the time to write out what it was I wanted to achieve. Nor the questions I would need to ask to reach my desired objective". "Why is that?" (You won't like this question!) "Because I haven't *made* the time to do it, OK!!". "Now, what's one thing you can do right now that would help you solve your problem so you can make all the phone calls that you need to make?" With some confidence, you can reply, "I can start with the objective I want to reach. Then I'll work on some questions, and even start writing a script I can use until I get more comfortable doing it from memory." Easy!!

And finally, you can ask friends and folks who do this kind of thing every day, for their suggestions and help to get over whatever hurdle you are facing. You can often get great support from others, who have at some time or another gone through similar experiences. No need to reinvent the wheel.

Other people are always willing to share with you what they have learned along the way.

Lights, Action, Camera.

Focusing is just like looking through a camera lens. You can see the view in the lens but it isn't clear. In fact, it's down right blurry. So when something isn't focused it is not clear what it is.

Now you can see that if you are not focused on success, the picture you hold of what success is will also be unclear and blurry. Before you focus the lens, you have to have an idea of what it is you want to have in the picture. Then just snap your photograph for "making a memory", as the Kodak people would say, for the album in your mind.

What is the picture for you? What image of success do you hold in your mind's eye? Is there one thing that comes to mind? And when you are standing in the picture, what would others say they see through the viewfinder?

It's an interesting point, but the object of our focus is what we have to view continually in our mind. Having just bought a camera recently, I know it will only take pictures of whatever is in the view finder when you press the button. Now, you knew that already. But what is the scene in your mind that you can see in the viewfinder of your life?

The mind, just like a camera, will only take pictures of whatever you focus on. If you only see yourself "trying" to do something that's exactly how the mind picture is going to develop. On the other hand, if you can visualize yourself as doing the goal, or even better yet, having actually achieved your desired goal, the mind will automatically develop that photo for you to keep up on the wall for you to admire.

Now Kodak and Fuji haven't yet developed a 3-D film for individual use, but you have! For you see the picture in your mind's eye in 3-D. It is as real as if you were actually there. And that is the magic of the mind.

Psychologists have repeatedly shown that the mind cannot tell the difference between a picture created in one's imagination and actually perceiving the real thing. You know how excited you get with the real thing. Well, you can start getting hyped up about that picture of your goal towards success.

Your Wonderful *MindAlter* Camera

I am sure Minolta won't mind my play on their name, but they saved the day for us on a recent vacation to Florida. The camera I had bought, whose brand name will remain nameless, just didn't work when we needed it. So we ended up having to go out and buy a new camera, and fortunately our new Minolta made wonderful memories of our trip and family moments.

Maybe your camera does the same thing as ours. It can put the date on the photograph when it was taken. You can do exactly the same thing with your mind using the telephoto focus lens into the future, and you can put the date on the picture when you want to achieve that goal.

This camera is made by *MindAlter*. Your *mind* can *alter* any part of the picture at any time. You can create more details and colour, and texture and sensory information. You can go back into your mind and alter the date if you have to. Sometimes goals pursued will create events that speed up the achievement of your desired goal.

Framing Your Favourite Pictures

When you take a particularly good picture it's kind of nice to get a good frame and put the photo somewhere in your home where you can enjoy the scene, people or object in the photograph. And this brings up an important point about getting the right frame and the right matting. You know, the matting is the coloured card that creates a border around the picture, all of which is held by the wooden or metal frame.

If you choose the wrong coloured matting and frame, it can virtually destroy the inherent beauty of the picture. Some people may purposely try to convince you to get the wrong matting. They will tell you that the goal within your picture is a little foolish. You know it will never work. Why don't you try and take another picture? Maybe you could let them take the picture so your goal will become their goal.

The very same picture with the right matting will actually have your goal stand out. A blue matting will bring out the blues. A green matting will bring out the greens in the land-scape of the house you want to buy. A positive matting will enhance the 3-D reality of your picture. Affirmative, optimistic statements surrounding the matting as your frame will allow you to focus on your masterpiece.

Viewing Your Gallery of Masterpieces

Now you can put your picture up on the wall and have it stand out in its perfect matting and gorgeous frame. Your goal image, packaged in a positive presentation, can now rank to be placed in the gallery where you will add other pictures of the things you want to have, be or do.

Once in a blue moon, I'll take one of my children who hadn't accompanied me the last time to our local art gallery. While some of the paintings or photographs can be quite abstract, there are others that really cause you to admire the colour choices, or the way the lighting and positioning of people and objects were done which cause you to focus in on one item or another.

And many of these paintings do not look too good up close. You really have to stand back to appreciate that all those strokes and blobs do make a picture, at a distance. It is amazing how an artist can create beauty one stroke at a time. They have to see the big picture in their minds while working up close everyday. You and I have to do the same thing with the success we want to achieve through our goals.

Stand back and take a good look at the picture of your life. What do you see? You must learn to visualize your success.

Visualizing Our Masterpieces

Art galleries always seem to be downtown, but you can usually purchase printed programs that have reproductions in miniature and give some history around the picture and the artist. Focusing on your journey towards success, you don't have to have the real thing before you in order to help motivate yourself towards your goal. Instead, you can visualize your focused pictures of your goal in your mind.

You can create your own printed program in your mind of the goals you want to achieve. This technique is known as visualization.

Visualization methods have been known by the ancients and are being practiced today by a wide variety of professionals, from psychologists, sports coaches, cancer patients, and of course...those pursuing their dreams.

I have always enjoyed the sports examples because they seem so concrete even though I am not an athletic individual. One year I was able to walk around the Canadian Open Golf Championship at Glen Abbey Golf Course in Oakville, Ontario.

I observed something I had only read about beforehand. When one of the big name pros hit a "bad" shot, say into a sand bunker, the golfer went through some kind of ritual which I will describe. You could see the pro not moving from where he had just hit the shot. He even lined up his club again as if he was going to hit another ball. Only there was no ball there. Now I know these guys aren't crazy. They make a lot of money at this game. But at first I couldn't figure out what was going on. What I later found out, was these pros did not want to have a negative image in their minds that could set up a self-fulfilling prophecy of the next shot being a "bad" one as well.

We've already learned from our chapter on focus on attitude, that our mind and then our body responds either positively or negatively to the dominant thought we hold in our minds. In a similar fashion our golf pros want to have a positive mindset before physically hitting the ball out of the bunker. They play a script in their heads that runs something like this, *"That's not like me (to have hit a ball into the bunker). I know I can do better. Next time I will."* With this positive view in the golfer's mind, they are all set to hit the ball.

Now the amazing thing is, that they go to that ball in the sand, take one swing at it and it seems to just float right up to the pin. In contrast, you may have seen a weekend golfer swing a dozen times at that ball in the bunker, only to bury themselves in the sand.

The key then, is to constantly visualize how you want things to be.

Sensesurround Visualization

Let me lead you through an exercise to make your visualization become *"sensesurround visualization"*.

In the traditional sense, visualization would really only cover the sense of vision. This way you would just repeatedly hold the image of what it is you want to achieve, whether it be something you want, something you want to become, or somewhere you want to be. You can help this sense along by having actual pictures of the desired goal. We'll be talking more about this under the next chapter on goals.

The visualization I am proposing utilizes all five senses and not just vision. It's just like those movie theatres that shake you up with their fantastic sound systems, and huge screens. I'll show you how it works.

First, like most relaxation exercises, get yourself into a comfortable chair and remove any tight clothing, belts, shoes, etc. Imagine yourself in your favourite chair. Vividly see the colour of the chair and feel the texture of the material. Now imagine a projection screen in front of you with a movie being shown of you and your visualized desire. Whether it's you in a role that you see yourself fulfilling, or hands on using an object you want to obtain, or even seeing yourself at a place you really want to be at.

With all the artistry and expertise of a movie producer, you incorporate all the visual effects you can into your movie. Wind machines can be used. Temperature can be controlled at a flick of a switch in this movie. Sounds of whatever is necessary, nature, machines, scripted parts from look-alike celebrities or special people you need, all of this will be there. You find yourself doing your part with all the behind the scene research and preparation that make it certain you will get an Oscar for your part. You will be doing any stunt work for your goal. You are the star!

And don't forget the sense of smell from books, to restaurants, to driving into the country. Whatever it will take to authenticate your movie, you are the producer so create a winner. No expense is too much for this movie because you will see it happen.

Believe me, this is a very powerful technique.

Creating My Own Movie

I was pursuing my graduate degree in communication disorders to be a speech-language pathologist. In the newspaper of the city we had previously lived in had appeared an announcement that a new hospital was being built that would include a rehabilitation facility which would serve individuals with brain injury and spinal cord injury. That was my dream!

I cut out that newspaper article and for the next few years it was posted smack centre of my bulletin board. It was in my face every minute I was studying at my desk at home. When nights were long, and courses became tough, all I had to do was look up and see that small piece of paper. That was where I was going to work!

You do a lot of clinical practice work as a speech-language pathologist and I was determined to get a practicum at the Rehabilitation Institute in Detroit. My clinical supervisor at the university told me she couldn't guarantee this for me. I just told her I had a job waiting for me and I had to have this experience.

I didn't get the placement I wanted for my first practicum. That's when you have to keep focusing. I had to keep looking at my newspaper article on my bulletin board. I could see myself working with the patients. I was back in that city with my young family. That was *my* job and I was going to get the next practicum where I needed it.

You have to wonder about a guy going around saying he is going to do a certain training practicum, and that he has a job in another city waiting for him, when you know full well that neither of them has even happened yet. But that is what I did. And that is what you are going to have to do if you want what you want badly enough.

The Rest Of The Story
.

It was six months before the new hospital would be officially opened where "my job" was waiting for me. I thought it would be a good time to touch base with my (soon to be) boss, to find out when I should submit my resume. I wasn't prepared for the answer. A letter arrived with the question, *"Could you please send me your resume at your earliest convenience."* I didn't have a resume!

And then I got the placement to the facility I had repeatedly told everyone I was going to get. I think my clinical supervisor was just as tickled to be able to arrange it for me.

Then I created what was really a *"visualized"* resume. Since I hadn't done the practicum yet with adults who had sustained brain injuries, I drafted a resume based on what other students had experienced who had done a similar practicum. Now I wasn't dishonest. My covering letter clearly stated that I would be doing my practicum that fall but that the attached resume included all the experience I knew I would get at completion.

Having interviewed and hired several employees since then, I can now see how that resume would have been viewed by any employer *"as if"* the job candidate had already acquired all the stated experience. I had created an image even in the employer's mind of my capabilities.

I mailed everything off. To my horror and ecstasy I received a letter back asking for an interview. I had only just begun my adult courses. What was I going to do with only three weeks away from the interview for *"my job"*? Remember the newspaper article? I had to focus on it hard. Did I want it badly enough?

The next three weeks found me studying every textbook dealing with adult communication disorders. I studied everything about the brain I could. I asked my fellow students all the treatment methods for working with people who had sustained brain injuries. I asked my professors for the latest applied clinical research articles they could find. My mind was swimming in a mass of confused information.

For someone who had not actually done an adult practicum, nor completed all the course work related to adult communication disorders, I think I was as prepared as anyone could be. The interview hardly touched this information. The questions were more on my life, why I had left employment to go to school as a married mature student, what my goals were, and why I wanted to work at this soon-to-be-unveiled new hospital. Well, she asked. I told her. And I told her about the newspaper clipping.

If you're wondering, I got the job. It was the only resume and job application I made. After all, it was my job.

After, my probationary period was over, my boss told me that she was amazed with all the contacting I had done so far in advance of the hospital opening and the precise follow up I had done after the interview. She had never met anyone more persistent in her life, she told me. When you're focused, you don't let go!

Turning Up The Intensity

I have to admit reliving that experience through writing this book brings back that excitement. And I know that is the key behind making your dreams come about. You have to continually relive the feelings in the movie and picture gallery of your mind. Those feelings and emotions have to be stoked up with hot burning coals that will drive up the heat.

Once you have the heat focused and directed, you have the intensity of drive to propel you into action. If there is no energy, strength or force behind your personal focus then there will be no belief or passion to see your dreams come to fruition. You have to stay focused to succeed.

Focus Points On Focus

Point #1: When you lose focus, as all of us do, ask yourself questions as to why. With repeated questioning and a collection of answers, do the most important answer and learn to focus on it until it is completed.

Point #2: Create the masterpiece picture of your success in your mind. Now frame it with the positive statements of you having achieved that success, e.g. "I am a successful speech-language pathologist".

Point #3: Visualizing what you want in your mind helps you to focus. It strengthens your belief and creates an attitude of expectancy. Take time out everyday to visualize on your success.

Point #4: Keep your dreams alive everyday. Relive them, think on them, see yourself succeeding and you will feel the dream come alive!

Point #5: Reflect on the various times in your life when you have been focused. Draw on the emotions and passion of that event. Now light the flame of that power and focus on your present goal!

THE POWER OF FOCUSING

While not directly mentioned in the previous pages, the question arises as to whether you can share your dream with others. Does it help or hinder?

You will find that as you achieve one focused goal after another, you will want to share more of your dreams with others. In the beginning, it may be wise to follow the suggestion of Zig Ziglar, who says if it is a "giving up" goal then you tell everyone and their mother. If it's a "going up" goal you tell only those closest to you who you love and can be trusted.

The reason for these differences are straightforward. When you want to *"give up"* something like smoking or losing weight, you need some cheerleaders out there to push you along and maybe slap your hand when you're steering in the wrong direction. On the other had, if you have a goal to *"go up"* to a management position that you aspire to, chances are pretty high there is someone else wanting the same thing. Broadcasting your dream in that kind of environment is only going to create tension and political infighting. Best to share this kind of goal with a trusted colleague, significant other or spouse.

Mind you, as you move along your journey towards success you will probably find that your dreams and goals are more unique. You are truly helping others at the same time as you are achieving your own personal fulfillment. As this happens, you will find that you can share your life dreams with others. In return, your friends will eventually start calling you with ideas and suggestions. This will add to your new found focus and bring you prosperity and accomplishment.

A Forever *Gr*attitude

One of the greatest things about moving towards your goals is that you end up meeting some of the nicest people in the world. Make sure you develop, what I call, a *G-R-attitude.* That's a *G*iving *R*ecognition attitude. Anytime someone helps you in any way at all, send them a thank you card as soon as you can.

So don't put this very important task off. Remember, to always put relationships ahead of achievements and tasks. You and I know that our "to-do" lists will always be there for us. But people may not always be around.

So go out and buy an ample supply of "thank you" cards and while you're at it stop by the post office and buy more stamps than you need. If you're like me you always seem to run out of stamps when you need them.

In my programs that I present on showing people how to give recognition to others, I show them a simple method to writing perfect thank you cards. You want the receiver to feel like a star so I have four points that follow the acronym based on the word *"STAR".*

Specific—Be real specific as to what it is that the person did for you and how it made a difference in your life. We often thank people for their actions but we rarely tell them why it made you feel good or how it helped you. People would really like to know how they made in a difference in your life.

Timely—Make time at the end of each day to write your thank you notes. Use those available moments in waiting rooms, on airplanes, or point blank right after the good deed was done. The closer to the occurrence your card can be sent, the greater the effect of your words.

Affirmative—You have to use positive, uplifting words of genuine gratitude and appreciation. This is no place for sarcasm nor for trying to sandwich in a criticism or two. And never, never, put the word "but" in any of your phrases. It only negates the whole message before the word.

Rewarding—Your thank you card must be the most rewarding communication they receive that day. And if you are going to send a token gift along with the card, the gift must be meaningful and represent in value the time, energy and effort that was put into the action they gave you.

And don't forget the telephone either. For people who are readily available on the phone, give them a quick call with no other purpose than to say thank you for something they have done for you. People are crying out to be appreciated for who they are and recognized for what they do. So make the time. You'll feel good too for having thanked someone who helped you along your journey to success.

Finally, whether by card, phone or in person, always ask the person who has helped you to let you know how you might be able to help them in any way. What goes around comes around. You reap what you sow. And so the law of the harvest is still in season.

Capturing The Dreams

As I have said before, I rarely ever remember my sleep dreams. But my success dreams are written down in my planner that goes everywhere with me (my wife promises she will bury it with me!). Another idea is to capture your dreams in a scrapbook of some kind.

All you have to do is to get a photo album or a traditional scrapbook to glue pictures in and go out and collect pictures and images of the dreams you want to achieve.

When we needed a new vehicle, and specifically a mini-van, and yet the bank account did not seem to be too accommodating, my wife went out and bought a toy mini-van. The side door opened and everything looked just like a miniature version of the real thing. I wrote on the side of this toy van the words "Faithmobile", because it was going to take a lot of faith to get this van. Then the toy van was placed on our bedroom dresser. We could see it every day when we got up and every night before going to bed. It was the focus of our prayers and our thoughts. Even the children got a kick out of calling the van we didn't yet have the "Faithmobile". After all, Batman has his Batmobile.

Funny thing when you focus. All I kept seeing on the road everywhere we went was mini-vans. And before you know it, an opportunity came about to purchase a second-hand vehicle that was used by an older couple, with very few miles on it, and in excellent condition.

Each of our vehicles has had a name of affection given to it from Charlie to Camille II, but it only seemed fitting that the real van that had been *"seen"* for several months on our dresser, should have one name.... Faithmobile! The children wouldn't have it any other way.

So if a new vehicle is on your dream list and you really need some focus work to do, go to your nearest dealer and ask them for brochures and books and cut out some pictures and put them in your "dream book". Or if you can, do as we did and buy a toy or model replica of the car you know belongs to you, and place it where you can see it everyday.

This is a skill that constantly needs to be practiced and developed. It is a fundamental requirement for turning belief into a focused energy. From it will come the power to act.

Meditation: A Time To Focus

Now before you think I'm getting too religious or anything, let me share with you first something I learned at university about focusing.

In my second year of university as a mature student, I made sure I got the courses and professors I wanted by doing a Consumer Report approach. I checked out the student evaluations of professors and then went and interviewed the "profs" before registering for my courses. This way I was choosing the education I got rather than have the system dictate to me. It paid off.

One psychology professor I interviewed was Dr. Alan Paivio, renowned in his research on memory and the learning of language. I asked him one of my standard questions: "What do you expect from your students?". I knew I was in for a challenge when he answered, "Perfection!".

I accepted the challenge. One of the course requirements was to replicate an experiment from the research textbooks. Then you had to write it up in scientific method style as to why the experiment worked or did not work. We had seven of these to do during the term and in total the mark counted for almost 40 percent of the course grade.

The first experiment went well. I remember labouring almost 24 hours straight on the write up. I submitted it and awaited an average to decent mark. Then I got the return shock to see a mark like 46 percent. I died! I sought out the tutorial teacher who marked the paper. Her only calming comment at the time was that I was not alone, yet she knew what Dr. Paivio expected.

Then she taught me a powerful lesson that helped me with my future papers in this course, and with all my courses thereafter. She said, "Each paper should only take you about 7 or 8 hours." When you have spent over three times as much time to get only 46 percent as a mark, you're probably with me in not being too believing of this woman. I told her, *"how could I do that when I already spent 24 hours on this paper and I got a lousy mark."* She re-affirmed that I had spent too much time on the assignment. She knew as a mature student and the willingness I had to learn and seek her out, that I was ready to hear the secret.

The secret, if you want to call it that, like all methods of success was a very simple one. She told me to stop doing the research first. She said go home and find a quiet place where you will be undisturbed. Relax your mind and body. Once accomplished, now start to just think on the experiment and keep asking yourself the question as to why it did or didn't work. She said it should take about half an hour, and when the reason comes, go to the library and find research that proves *your* idea rather than regurgitating all the research that explained the rationale for the original experiment.

I remember the second experiment very well. It didn't work according to the psychologist who had expounded the theories behind it. Now it was my job to explain why it hadn't worked. It was kind of weird to go downstairs to our unfinished basement and sit in a chair and just think. But that's exactly what I did. And I tell you that within half an hour I could "see" why the experiment had failed. Like the ancient Greek, Archimedes, who ran through the streets shouting "Eureka", I ran upstairs shouting, *"I've got it! I've got it!"*. Then I ran to the library and was easily able to find articles that substantiated my ideas rather than what other psychologists had claimed.

The paper was completed within seven hours. The mark? You can bet I was anxious to get the paper back. Yet somehow I knew I had discovered something I had never experienced before. I was optimistic that this fresh approach had turned on some juices in my brain that had lain dormant. Well, I got 86 percent. The tutor smiled at me and I nodded and later shared with her the merits of meditating.

Very few students got high marks on papers in that course. I shared with as many as I could what our tutor had taught me.

Many thought I was crazy. But I saw a few believers see the light as I consistently stayed in the high eighties with my marks.

Hopefully, you can see some similar ideas you can apply to focusing on your personal and professional goals and dreams. Take just one of your dreams and invest half an hour of your time. Give your dream the luxury of your undivided attention and ask yourself the questions as to how to achieve. Even if you can only give ten or fifteen minutes to this exercise, begin today to do it. Many of the answers to your dreams are inside of you. You just need to tap the inner mine of wealth that is buried inside.

Spiritual Reflections

I've shared with you before that I wouldn't be anywhere near where I am in life, if it wasn't for my faith in my Heavenly Father and Jesus Christ. Now whether you believe in God, or a spiritual Higher Power or not, I would ask you not to throw out the idea of praying or meditating upon the ideas that you have to achieve success. I find that when your dreams are directed at wanting to help other people the Laws of the Universe unveil themselves to help you in ways that you could never do on your own.

The most repeated admonition in the Bible is to *ask!* It was Jesus Christ who told us to ask, seek, and knock. Author and management consultant, Joe Batten, says if you take the first letters of those three words:– **a**sk, **s**eek, **k**nock – you actually get the word "ask". So don't hesitate to ask and be prepared to work as if everything depended on you, and pray as if everything depended upon the Lord.

For those of you who believe in prayer or have experienced the miracles of answers, remember to express your gratitude to Him who has given you that blessing. Remember to give in return something to your community at large. Ask in your moments of meditation as to how you can help someone else reach their dreams. The answers will come, and often not while you are reflecting. You will be about your business when a prompting will come to call a particular person for no reason at all. Or you may be reading a magazine and feel impressed to send a copy of the article to someone on your mind. Then again, you may just go and do something for someone and brighten up their day.

The key is to continually focus on what it is you want to achieve. To believe without any hint of doubt that you can succeed. Repeatedly work on the thoughts in your mind to create the right attitude that will help you reach the goals you have set for yourself. These are the skills for unlocking the art and practice of focusing.

Focus Points On Focus

Point #1: Share your goals with others to help with focusing. Remember Zig Ziglar's advice. If it's a *"give up"* goal tell everyone; if it's a *"going up"* goal tell only your trustworthy supporters.

Point #2: Enjoy the thrill of succeeding by focusing on those who help you. Thank everyone who adds in some small or big way to your success. Get a supply of thank you cards and use them today!

Point #3: Create your own *"dream album"* by buying a photo album and collecting pictures that represent your dreams and focuses of success. Look at your album everyday and focus on each page.

Point #4: Try meditation to find answers, ideas, and alternatives to make your breakthrough to success. Many of the major scientific, financial and entrepreneurial successes have come from the quiet solitude of meditation. You'll be amazed at what you can achieve.

Point #5: Putting a spiritual root to belief, attitude, and focusing on the right things, along with meditation and prayer, creates the powerful force of faith. Apply spiritual principles to your balance of focusing on success.

Point #6: No matter what others may think, or what distractions around you may compete for your attention, STAY FOCUSED!

MAKING YOUR GOALS REAL

Your goals are more than just wishes because you have to make them come true. And yet, there is no doubt in my mind that once you focus on setting and achieving your goals a magic attraction brings success to you.

You are reading the words of someone who is a student of goal setting and achieving. It is an area with which I continue to learn. Over the years I have subscribed to many systems of setting goals. There have been occasions where I have been extremely focused on my goals. At other times I have lost my direction and momentum.

The key is to dream big, keep it simple, start small, and work on it every day.

A few years ago, I was approached by a teleconferencing company to create a presentation on goal setting. My contact had a vision of selling a workbook to each participant at every site. Could I do this? Sure, was my immediate response. Then came those discomforting words of how they would need them within three weeks in order to start shipping them out as people registered.

I'll never forget those three weeks. I was working my full-time job during the day. At night I worked on the workbook. My resistance was down and I came down with the worst case of 'flu I'd ever had. I had to sleep the fever off. Then it was back to the writing.

After the writing was done, it was a matter of getting the draft to the printer, shrink wrapping the workbooks into packages of five, and drop shipping them to the site of the teleconferencing company. And so within three weeks and one day I saw a published workbook being sold to the public.

Even though I published the workbook on goal setting, I realized I had much to learn about achieving goals. Some of these lessons I'll share along the way.

Making The Dream Come True

You have probably worked in some business or organization that has made a big deal about having a strategic plan. Absolutely hours of individual and group thinking goes into the creation of these documents. Hopefully this plan will help guide that organization towards its crafted destiny.

How much time have you invested in strategizing your life? Do you know where you're going? What about your next year? How about the next five or ten years? Planning as much of the future as is in your control, is an essential strategy utilized by many of the successful people throughout the world.

By learning how to plan and set goals, you will discover some of the great wealth of resources buried within you. Some of these wonderful talents are just below the surface and have been waiting for years to be mined and refined. When you add to these resources a meaningful purpose or mission like we have discussed before, you can't help but be committed to improving your personal and professional life.

Get It Down And Get It Going

You have got to realize and accept the fact, that within you is the very passion you need to burn up a pathway to achieving your desired purpose in life. You will need to think and dream big. Dream of the goals you have always wanted to see come true. Let go of the thoughts and words from others who have told you it cannot be done. Get rid of the self-limiting thoughts and behaviours that you have imposed upon yourself and soar towards success. Break down the barriers of past defeat and failures. Get ready to write down the goals that will make you stretch beyond where you are now. Prepare yourself to succeed at the goals you will choose.

The harsh reality is that many will never get beyond the act of dreaming. They forget one very simple step that would get them further than most people even imagine. You have got to write it down! Because if you do not write it down then you are just wishing your life away.

So it's decision time. You are going to have to make a decision to do something if you really want to focus on success. Are you all talk about your goals or do you really want to achieve them? The choice is all yours!

Go on. Go get a pen or pencil. It is your tool towards success.

Commit to disciplining yourself and completing the different exercises along the way that will help you progress in your personal life planning. And here is the tricky part to the commitment. See if you can complete the exercises before moving on. This way you can maintain the same feelings you had while reading the chapter as you put pen to paper. It's much harder to feel the same intensity of motivation if you just keep reading and then go back to the exercises later on. Decide to do it!

Planning The Journey
Of A Lifetime

You will find that planning your life is like planning a summer vacation. The irony is that we often put more time into a two or three week vacation than we do into the many years that life provides us with.

Let's pretend you want to go to Vancouver, British Columbia or San Francisco, California. (If you haven't guessed it already, I live in the East!). Your first step will probably be to visit your favourite travel agent or automobile association to get travel guides, maps and brochures.

We'll target going to Vancouver because my wife would really like to take the family out to where she went to university. With those scenic, colourful pictures and the maps in hand, you are beginning to get excited. The adrenaline juices are surging and you are raring to go.

So now that you know where it is where you want to go, just work your way back to your destination point. If you have a highlighter to trace your steps, you already have the route you can use on your trip.

You have probably had similar experiences on earlier holidays. Well, goal setting is exactly the same. First, you will have to decide where it is you want to go. This will be your goal. Then you have to write out a written picture of your goal so that you have a scenic image that gets you all excited about starting the journey. The power of visualization and having a written motivator of your destination is unbelievable. For your next step, you just work your way backwards on a time-line and figure out the route, or action plans, you will take to reach your destination.

You are probably familiar with the Chinese proverb that states, *"a journey of a thousand miles begins with a single step"*. Let me bring you up to speed with a twentieth century version from no other than Michael Jordan. In his inspirational book on the pursuit of excellence, titled *I Can't Accept Not*

Trying, Michael offers the advice of *"Step by step. I can't see any other way of accomplishing anything."* So take the step. One at a time. And watch the journey begin.

The Journey Begins

You may be like many others who simply justify not planning with statements like, "How can I plan the future? I can hardly manage to keep on top of one day at a time!". And with all the uncertainty in today's world, many are puzzled by such a suggestion and ask, "How can I control the future? Everything keeps changing."

Let me answer your concerns. When you have a purpose in life that is bigger than you are, you value your time more than any other commodity that life gives you. You will find that those who are truly successful in life and not just in material possessions, have learned to discipline themselves to stay in charge of each day.

When you plan your life you will see the miracle of serendipity, those unforeseen opportunities that come when you didn't plan them, appear before your very eyes. You will find by planning your life, the big picture, that the day to day painting of the details actually becomes more exciting and easier to manage. Your life plan begins to act as a North Star to guide you over the rough seas of life that will inevitably wash their effects upon you.

Some of my friends have told me that by planning out your life, you end up being too structured with no freedom to enjoy life. On the contrary, it's a very funny thing about life planning and setting your goals. The more you can structure the course or direction of your life, the easier it is to handle and steer around the changes that life throws at you.

It is the unexpected opportunities that come before us that make the journey of life all the more interesting. By having a master plan you can see if the new idea is a fit with your purpose, does it fall into the present plan, or are you willing to create a whole new plan because of the value this re-direction would bring.

By no surprise to you, those who have succeeded in any major personal or professional endeavour have had lots of goals. They have them written down and posted up on their walls. Somehow their goals are constantly before their eyes and re-affirmed in their minds.

Make goal setting and achieving them a priority in your life. You will discover for yourself that the greatest reason for strategizing your life is to be able to fully give of yourself, to use your talents and abilities to their fullest. You will experience the joy of making a difference in the lives around you and contributing to making the world a better place to be in. And you can do all this by planning to do whatever it is that makes you the happiest.

A Personal Guarantee

If you will make the time to complete each exercise that will help you create your strategic life plan of goals, and then carefully and systematically carry out each of your action plans, step by step, I guarantee you will see the realization of many of your goals and experience an untold satisfaction with your life. If you find all of these ideas towards goal setting and how to achieve them don't bring you an increase in success, then send the book back to me and I'll refund the cost of the book.

Now it is true that theoretically you could end up only achieving fifty percent of your written goals because of the roadblocks and detours that happen along the way. But you compare that level of achievement with the average person on the street and you'll still be way ahead of the whole bunch.

Do you know the reason why? They have no goals at all. And at the same time, if you only achieve fifty percent of the goals you had written down, you have probably accomplished more goals than you have ever done before. At this rate alone you will surpass in one year what the average person only dreams of in a lifetime. Remember, a dream is only a wish unless it is written down.

Once you've written it down, it's a goal!

Focusing On The Destination

Do you recall my hospital job and the newspaper clipping that kept me focused? It took me five and a half years to complete the education I needed to get that job. By having my goals written down and a passion to propel myself forward, it helped me to overcome the negative comments and criticisms that come from friends, co-workers, and even family.

Many people thought I was crazy to leave the "secure" job I had in the oil industry. Within seven years that job was gone. And yet there were others who took me aside and shared these words, "I wish I could do what you're doing." The answer of course is that they could. But they didn't believe they could do it. It was too big a risk. There were too many people saying it couldn't be done.

Why do those closest to us seem to put us down when we talk about achieving goals? There can be many reasons. Some of the most common include fear, jealousy, disbelief, and apathy. People can fear things that appear to be stable and in control, which is exactly what you'll be as you get your goals down on paper and start making them happen. Your friends and family may show some signs of jealousy as they see you actually achieve things they have secretly wanted to do as well. There will be a few in the crowd that disbelieve that goals will even get you somewhere. And then there are others who display a general apathy about being able to do anything worthwhile with life anyways.

When you face these kind of challenges head on, and trust me they will come, remember who you really are and that you are entering that elite and successful world of those who write their goals down on paper. You are becoming a member of the magical few where you can change the world with your ideas and hard work.

More importantly, you will see yourself doing and achieving what had seemed impossible—the reaching of personally meaningful goals. This is the true definition of success.

Appraising Your Priceless Resources

A typical perception of how goals are made is based on the New Year's resolutions that get made on the first day of the new year and are broken before the end of the month. Take a visit to any fitness club in the beginning of January to see the truth of this fact. You'll see lots of people starting out strong and then the numbers dwindle by the end of the month. It's the difference between a wish and a goal.

To achieve the goals you are going to be writing down, it's important to acknowledge some key factors about yourself. You must accept that you came into this world equipped with many worthwhile talents, skills, and special characteristics that make you all that you are. Now you may feel a little embarrassed thinking about these things. You may even try to deny that you have such resources available to you.

You are not alone in your feelings. For many years some of you have been told only what you cannot do and never what you can do. Lines like, "Oh, you'll never amount to anything!" are commonly thrown around. These negative labels can often remain fixed to us like a ball and chain never to be removed even up through our adult years. You may still be struggling with the destructive effects of such labeling. These incorrect descriptions can even influence you to believe that you have no talents. When this happens you may end up always trying to please others because you believe you have no innate abilities to achieve anything on your own merit.

What you need to do is bury these feeling of inadequacy deep in the ground outside of your home. Disregard any negative criticisms and comments from others because they don't know what you have inside of you. They only see a reflection of the outside of you. Your potential is within. Believe in yourself and trust your inner sense of your own worth. It is real and it is true!

Take a look at your own Personal Resource Account on the next page and see what the balance is. To see the balance you are going to have to put some entries in first.

Under the Talents column, write down all the special talents with which you have already been blessed. Don't worry if they are not fully developed talents or not, just make sure you list them. They could be anything from a talent for writing, a love of reading, musical talents with instruments or your voice, perhaps you are great at getting along with people. You could be a great public speaker, maybe you love animals, no matter how big or small your talents may be, write them down. Take your time on this column. Think carefully of the sharing of talents you have made over the years. There is no rush with this exercise.

Move on to the Skills column of your Personal Resource Account. If you again stop to think about your life so far, you will see you have learned many skills that have enabled you to find and maintain your employment. These skills also allow you to contribute to and enjoy many areas of your personal life. This is not a time to be bashful. Acknowledge the skills you have acquired and write them down in your Personal Resource Account. You may have learned on the job to deal with interpersonal conflict, how to cook specialty foods, how to word process, know a complex problem solving method, fix a car, all the many wonderful variety of skills that do not come from an innate talent, but purely from the experience of learning.

So take the time now to add your Skills to your Personal Resource Account on the next page, and take a good look at what you are really worth. You really are a priceless commodity, my friend!

PERSONAL RESOURCE ACCOUNT

TALENTS	SKILLS	CHARACTERISTICS

Remember: Talents X Skills X Characteristics = Endless Possibilities

There are also some special characteristics about yourself that are worth noting and adding to your expanding account book. These characteristics are the unique qualities that make you who you are. They make you a valuable person so make sure you recall them.

So now pick up your pen and pencil and move over to the Characteristics column in your Personal Resource Account to complete the bookkeeping of your life. Record the positive and inspiring characteristics about you. Make the time to think about the statements that you have heard other people say to describe you. These are the unmistakable characteristics that when mentioned along side your name has everyone nodding their heads in agreement. Maybe someone has said you are a patient individual, that you show a lot of understanding towards others, you are always positive and happy, or some other characteristic. Deep down you know you have these characteristics. You are just going to have to acknowledge them whether you like it or not. Get them down in your account book.

Some of you may get stuck filling up the columns in your Personal Resource Account. No problem, ask someone who knows you well to share their positive perceptions of you. Ask them how they or others describe you. It may seem a little difficult to go around asking people about yourself, but take the time to explain what you are doing and most people will be pleased to help. Just go and ask!

Stand Back, And Take
A Look At *You!*

Here you have your resources before you. You look great on paper! The sum total is really a multiplication job. You have to multiply your talents times your skills and multiply that by your characteristics in order to get the result of endless possibilities. The reason you have to multiply your resources is because you may not have combined these resources to their fullest potential. Now imagine the possibilities if you use them all towards your goals for success.

And that's the beauty of setting goals. You can never quite tell what the outcome will be when you start on the road to achieving your goals. But one thing is for sure, the results will be far greater than you first imagined.

The successful achievement of your goals will naturally depend on how well you utilize your identified resources. As in all aspects of life, the choice is in your hands as to how you will best use these resources. You can choose whatever direction in life you want. What you must solidly ingrain into your mind is that you cannot choose what the consequences will be. The outcomes you want to obtain are bound to the Laws of the Universe. If you want to achieve a certain goal in life, you must be prepared to pay whatever the price of admission is through work, discipline, time and energy that will see your dream become reality.

Creating A Statement Of Purpose

We talked earlier about knowing what it is that moves you and inspires you to live and breathe life into your world. In order to commence your new journey towards a successful life, you have to know what purpose you want to reach in life. In other words, what is the passion that turns you on?

There are too many people in our world today who have no idea where they are going or what it is they want in life. They set their ship to sea with every intention of enjoying a trip around life, but they have no rudder to steer them and no sails to catch the wind that will propel them forward.

Maybe you have set goals before and not achieved them. Many people wonder why they lack the steam and the perseverance to continue and see their goals accomplished. The answer comes in the words of the noted British politician Benjamin Disraeli who clearly stated, *"the secret of success is constancy of purpose"*. I like that. For if you want to succeed, you've got to stick to what you believe in.

Having a purpose that burns within you can give you the level of commitment that will help you to continue when everything around you appears to be caving in. It will give you the staying power to complete the tasks that must be done in order to succeed, even when you do not feel like doing them. A statement of purpose will give you the reason "why" for reaching the goals you'll soon be writing down.

Do not expect your statement of purpose to just fall into place right away. You may find it requiring several rewrites before you are totally satisfied. It may even take several weeks or months before it is in its finished form. But we cannot wait to get moving, so get something down, however imperfect, that captures the essence of your purpose. The goal with your purpose statement is to get it down. You can always get it "right" later.

Before doing some structured exercises to create your own personal purpose statement, you may find it worthwhile to answer some questions and discover some more about yourself.

Answer the following questions about yourself as candidly and as fully as possible.

• What kind of life do you envision yourself living if you had everything you needed to be able to live that way?

_____

_____

_____

_____

_____

_____

_____

- What kind of work or contribution to society have you always wished you could be doing? Remember your Personal Resource Account of talents, skills and characteristics.

_____

_____

_____

_____

_____

_____

_____

- How would your family relationships and friendships be better if your life was going the way you wish it could be?

_____

_____

_____

_____

_____

_____

_____

- How do you want people to remember you when you pass away from this life?

_____

_____

_____

_____

_____

_____

_____

Hopefully, these questions will cause you to do some serious and reflective thinking on the real meaning of life and where you see yourself being able to make a difference. Your thoughts will eventually come together to create your own life purpose.

Remember the most important part of your life purpose which was shared with you earlier. Your life purpose should indicate "the greatest use of life, is to so live your life, that the use of your life, will outlive your life." Read that again. I found this quote somewhere and it really does make sense. For when you have discovered a life mission that fulfills this greater purpose, you will have found more of yourself to give. You will also have unleashed the most powerful known source of motivation available to mankind that can make you a successful man or woman.

Let's take a look at a format for creating your personal purpose statement that very much mirrors the structure used to design a mission statement for a business or organization.

The most important action behind your purpose statement is to first reflect. What are you going to do to help other people? Notice that in looking at your purpose in this way you focus on someone else and not yourself. If there is ever a secret to success, it is in the helping of others to reach their goals. By doing this you will achieve the greatest degree of success for yourself.

Here are a few building blocks for the creation of your purpose statement. Complete the following directions and then we'll put them together at the end.

1. Write down one or several action verbs that describe what it is you want to do to help others.

_____
_____
_____
_____
_____

2. Write down as specifically as you can the description of the group, kind, or type of people you want to serve.

_____

_____

_____

_____

_____

3. Write down by what means you will help people by describing a few of the talents, skills, and characteristics you plan to use.

_____

_____

_____

_____

_____

4. What do you want these wonderful people to achieve through your help?

_____

_____

_____

_____

_____

My own purpose statement has changed a few times over the years. I have redefined my direction as life became clearer as I moved towards achieving the goals I had written down . It is important to be flexible and to rediscover your life purpose.

Right now, my purpose statement is as follows:

"My purpose statement is to show people how to recognize and appreciate their own, and others', great worth and potential, in their personal, family and business lives, through speaking, writing and consulting."

So looking back at the previous questions, you can see the answers I must have written. For the verbs that were essential to me, the words "show", "recognize" and "appreciate" stood out. As for the kind of people, I have left mine very general other than adding "in their personal, family and business lives". And of course, my method for providing this purpose in life is through my talents of speaking and the skills of writing and consulting. This enables these people to be able to recognize "their great worth and potential." You'll see that my statement of purpose does not follow the exact order shown below, but the content is the same. You can play around with yours *once* you have it down.

Look at the following format and use the answers from your statements above to try your hand at crafting a purpose statement.

My purpose in life is to

_____

(write the action words you identified)
_____

(describe the type of people you will help)

by: _____

(list the talents, skills or characteristics you will use)

so that: _____

(identify what these people will achieve with your help)

_____

Living With Purpose

Keep playing around with your purpose statement until it *"feels"* right for you. This is you. It is what you are all about. It's what you want to be and what your future life will be like as you focus constantly on your purpose in life. You now have your source of power to propel you in achieving your goals.

Dr. Robert H. Schuller the creator of "possibility thinking" and minister of the renowned Crystal Cathedral, shares a powerful message from Coretta King, the widow of Dr. Martin Luther King in his book *Success Is Never Ending... Failure is Never Final.* He asked Coretta King where she got her dream from. Her reply was that she got her dream while attending Antioch College which was founded by Horace Mann. History records that Horace Mann told the first graduating class at Antioch in the late 1850s these motivating words, *"Be ashamed to die until you've won some victory for humanity."* Is it any wonder that the cause of Dr. King's "I have a dream", which was his personal life purpose, would see itself continuing to live on after he died through his wife.

Make sure your purpose is big enough to live for and strong enough to die for too!

Like Peter Phelps on the popular TV show *Mission Impossible,* you also have to answer the challenge of *"your mission, should you decide to accept."* The neat thing is that you have chosen your mission. When you have had a say in something there is always more ownership and commitment to do whatever goal or plan you have set for yourself. Now all you have to do is totally "accept" your mission and purpose in life. Start creating those goals that are just busting to come out of you, and get them down on paper!

Now that you have your purpose statement defined and written out, memorize it and repeat it to yourself often. You have to let it go from your mind and sink into your heart. With a purpose as your constant guide you can learn to really focus.

Taking A Look At
Your "Life Line"

With your life purpose statement now in hand, you must now become your own futurist. You will not have a crystal ball to do this. Neither will you be seeking out a palm reader. But you will be examining your own personal "Life Line".

Your "Life Line" is a helpful tool you can use to examine your life and figure out what major events you can anticipate in your life. Furthermore, since our own life is intertwined in the relationships of our spouse, partner, children, and even parents, you can also take a look at projecting a picture of your life with theirs.

This process helps you to realize the ages you and everyone else will be at over the next five year period. By carrying out this exercise you will seriously reflect on what significant ages or events should be happening over the next five years. This allows your "Life Plan" sheet to be a great beginning step to seeing the end point of a five year journey and focusing on relationships before you zero in on achievements.

The instructions are straightforward for completing your "Life Line" on page 105. Put in the correct year. I'm no longer writing "19__" because the years starting in 2000 are just around the corner. Write your name under the "name" column in the first row. If there are other people in your life that you need to consider in your plans, write their names down one name per row. When you have a spouse or partner and some children it's pretty effective to write the names down in descending chronological order by age.

You'll notice that at the top of each year block is marked off like a ruler with three lines making four equal divisions. Each division represents three months of each year. So the lines mark out the third, sixth and ninth months.

All you have to do is plot where your birthday would fall in each year box according to the month markers. Just mark your birthday's occurrence with an "X" in each year block. Underneath each "X" indicate the respective age for that year. Go ahead and do the same procedure for all family members and significant others as you have listed.

A brief example of how your "Life Line" could start off is shown below.

Name	Year _____	Year _____
Age JOHN	X 28 Have medical	X 29 Learn to swim
Age ANNE	X 30 Arrange surprise party	X 31 Remember 10th year since graduated.

With names, birthdates and ages all plotted for yourself and family, see if there are any significant events coming up in each person's life in any of the five years. Maybe an anniversary is coming up, time for a surprise party, entering teenage years, toilet training, starting school, teaching someone to drive, making time to play basketball with a child, or taking a course.

So, on the following page take the time to plot you, your family and/or significant people in your life. Then fill in the special events and life markers associated with yourself and the people you have identified.

Sometimes you just need to stop and look into the future to realize some special times would drift away unless you make time to catch them and hold on. By examining your "Life Line" you will be able to anticipate these significant events in

YOUR PERSONAL "LIFELINE"©

Name	YEAR:	YEAR:	YEAR:	YEAR:	YEAR:
Age					
Age					
Age					
Age					
Age					
Age					

your own and others' lives and plan to do something about it. This will allow you to build relationships and make special memories.

Writing Down The Goals
You've Always Wanted

Remember your destination of Vancouver, B.C. or San Diego, California? That is where you want to go to no matter where in the world you are right now. You are almost ready to plan out the goals you've always wanted to achieve in life. You have your personal purpose statement to guide you and your "Life Line" to help you stay on track of those important milestones in the next five years.

It's time to dream again of your goals. Practice in your mind's eye by closing your eyes and imagine you're rubbing Aladdins's magic lamp. You can wish for anything you want in any aspect of your life. The only restriction is that you must never violate another's rights with your wish. The genie is prepared to grant you your wishes. And trust me, this is the traditional live genie, not the cartoon version. Try to picture for a few minutes what you would have in your possessions, what you would be doing in your life everyday, what roles you would be living, where you would be, and how you would be contributing to the world to make it a better place.

Open your eyes. Take a deep breath and then breathe out. Turn and take a look at your Dream List on the next page. There are 101 spots for you to fill in just like a 1001 Arabian Nights from Aladdin's tales. Fill in all the things you would wish to have, the relationships you want to build, positions to achieve, people to meet, places to go, and experiences to encounter.

Keep a positive and open mind to your ideas. Break down the limitations of the past and the negative statements from those around you. Let your mind brainstorm away and write down as many of your wishful goals as you can. Dream big!

Write down your goals and not someone else's. Allow each idea to connect to the next goal on your list. Branch off in any direction you choose from family to career, from vacation spots to things to learn. Just keep writing!

YOUR 101 GOAL DREAM LIST

The next few pages are set aside for all the dreams you have ever wanted to see fulfilled. Find a quiet place where you will not be disturbed. Close your eyes and for several minutes meditate and imagine all the things you really want to have, to be or to do. Even places you want to go to. Now, write without stopping for as long as you can. Come back as often as you can the same day, the next day, or whenever a dream comes or a goal you want to reach. Do this until all 101 spots are filled. You can do it. Just dream! Evaluate your goals only after all 101 goals are written down.

No.	Write your goals down here	"Really want it" Check here	Year to be achieved 1, 2, 3 ,4, 5 →
		Your 101 Goal Dream List	
		Evaluation of Goals	
1			
2			
3			
4			
5			
6			
7			
8			

No.	Write your goals down here	"Really want it" Check here	Year to be achieved 1, 2, 3 ,4, 5 →
	Your 101 Goal Dream List		
		Evaluation of Goals	
9			
10			
11			
12			
13			
14			
15			
16			
17			
18			
19			
20			
21			
22			
23			
24			
25			
26			
27			

No.	Write your goals down here	"Really want it" Check here	Year to be achieved 1, 2, 3 ,4, 5 →
		Evaluation of Goals	
28			
29			
30			
31			
32			
33			
34			
35			
36			
37			
38			
39			
40			
41			
42			
43			
44			
45			
46			

Your 101 Goal Dream List

No.	Write your goals down here	"Really want it" Check here	Year to be achieved 1, 2, 3 ,4, 5 →
**Your 101 Goal Dream List**			
		Evaluation of Goals	
47			
48			
49			
50			
51			
52			
53			
54			
55			
56			
57			
58			
59			
60			
61			
62			
63			
64			
65			

		Evaluation of Goals	
No.	Write your goals down here	"Really want it" Check here	Year to be achieved 1, 2, 3 ,4, 5 →
66			
67			
68			
69			
70			
71			
72			
73			
74			
75			
76			
77			
78			
79			
80			
81			
82			
83			
84			

Your 101 Goal Dream List

No.	Write your goals down here	"Really want it" Check here	Year to be achieved 1, 2, 3 ,4, 5 →
85			
86			
87			
88			
89			
90			
91			
92			
93			
94			
95			
96			
97			
98			
99			
100			
101			

Your 101 Goal Dream List

Evaluation of Goals

...And Just For Good Measure!

Your 101 Goal Dream List			
		Evaluation of Goals	
No.	**Write your goals down here**	**"Really want it" Check here**	**Year to be achieved 1, 2, 3 ,4, 5 →**
102			
103			
104			
105			
106			
107			
108			
109			
110			

These are just some of the goals you will achieve during your lifetime!

The first time I followed this idea sparked by Mark Victor Hansen's book *Dare To Win*, it took me forever to complete the list. Strive to put a good half-hour to an hour into this to get as much good stuff down as you can. Then come back to it every day to complete the list. I redid my list just recently and now I am able to fill in the 101 spots in no time at all. It just takes practice in dreaming. I hereby give you permission to dream the goals of a lifetime.

What you have just done is one of the most important exercises to make your dreams come true. With your purpose statement, your "Life Line", and now your dream list of goals, you are now ready to decide which goals you will work on right now.

YOUGOTTAWANNA!

Before you think that's a North American Indian name, take a good look and you'll see it's actually made up of three words: You—Gotta—Wanna. This is where you are going to evaluate your goals. And the first step is to check off all the goals that you really, honest to goodness want. That's why I am saying you really "gotta wanna" have this goal with all your heart, mind and soul! Just check off in the *"Really Want It"* column of your 101 goals, those you are willing to apply self-discipline, hard work, and an all around willingness to pay the price and go the distance to achieve.

The next step is to identify which goals you are prepared to commit to and achieve within the next year. Go down the right hand *"Year To Be Achieved"* column and and indicate with a number *"1"* the goals you want to achieve this year.

For the other goals you really want to work on, just not this year, go back and have another look to make sure you haven't missed any for *this* year. Once you have done this, examine the remaining goals and approximate when you think you will get them accomplished and write down 2, 3, 4, or 5 to represent the year you want to complete that goal. Use an arrow for goals you think are beyond five years.

Evaluating Your Goals

Because goal setting is a serious business, you should take a closer look at the goals you have checked and placed a number 1 beside. These goals are the ones you are saying you really want to achieve within the next twelve months. Focus on each of the goals and see if you are prepared to invest your time and energy into making them happen. Now ask yourself the following questions.

What will I benefit from achieving this goal? You have to be able to answer the "what's in it for me" question for working on this goal. If the motivation is not big enough or strong enough to get you over the hard times, the late nights, or distractions of life, the goal is not worth shooting for. For some of your relationship goals the benefits could be an ever improving friendship and relationship with your spouse, and love and harmony with your children. In some of your business focused goals, the benefits may be in creating your own financial independence and being able to assist others in ways that will enable them to be self-reliant and happy.

What are some possible obstacles that I must overcome to reach this goal? You may have heard of negative preparation. That's what you are doing by answering this question. What problems, detours, challenges do you need to be prepared for? By planning ahead with these answers you can anticipate what you will have to do to reach your goal. Often the biggest challenge in relationship goals is ourselves!

Other obstacles may be recognizing your priorities and organizing yourself, or overcoming your past without dwelling on it. For the more achievement oriented goals it may be a limitation of finances and lack of knowledge and experience in marketing, or some other skill. Answers to this question get you ready for the next question.

What experience, knowledge or help might I need to achieve this goal? This takes away the negative perspective of obstacles and turns them right side up by looking at the positive solutions to the potential problems. In improving a marriage relationship, listening to one's partner is a great way to learn! There are also some wonderful books and videotapes that inspire new thoughts and ideas. For your children you must continually be learning about self-esteem and how to communicate better. Again discussion with your spouse, friends, professionals and religious leaders, as well as printed, audio- and videotaped materials can provide great support. In the business side of things you may need to learn how to do a business plan. Colleges often provide courses on business startup strategies. Banks can provide you with literature and computer discs to do a business plan. And touch base with your professional or trade association for reference material and peer support.

What is my plan for getting the goal completed? This is where you have to get out of the chair, if you need to leave it, or into the chair in my case when I started writing this book. Write down at least five things you need to do to get your goal in motion. Sometimes a goal can seem totally overwhelming, but follow Alan Lakein's philosophy of the "Swiss Cheese Effect" which he outlines in his book *How To Get Control of Your Time And Your Life.* Just like the multiple little holes in Swiss cheese, you need to tackle your plan in bite sized attempts. Maybe you have to do a flow chart to help you see all the steps to complete. This provides a natural chronological order to follow your plan. It's also fun to take the first step and tick it off when it's done, and then move on to the next action.

What is the date by which I will reach my goal? Each goal has to have a target date for which you are going to do your utmost to reach. Remember you are competing only against yourself. The date should be challenging but do-able. And should you miss the date, just take a good look at what you *have* done and don't whip yourself on what you *haven't* done. You'll be well on your way to accomplishing your goal so don't sweat a small, or long delay for that matter, when you've made it so far. Having a date becomes a personal challenge and also helps you to do some course correction or pulling-up-of-socks if needed.

What measure can I use to evaluate my progress towards my goal? I don't know about you but some of these goals can appear impossible at first glance. Now I want you to know I believe that nothing is impossible! The best approach is to have lots of little successes you can more easily aim for. With my book, it was so many pages a day or so much time spent on the computer. You may have so many hours studying for a course each night, or so much money saved up towards a house each month, whatever the measure break it up into smaller increments so you can see yourself succeeding. There is nothing like success to breed more success.

When you have taken a good long look at each of your goals using these questions you are going to have to make a hard choice and focus.

Over the years I have personally struggled with setting and then achieving my goals. I won't deny that maintaining the self-discipline to keep up with some goals, or keeping the attitude burning at full steam is not always easy. And it has only been recently that I have realized the issue of focusing has made all the difference for me. And that's what I am recommending you now do with your goals.

What I have done is chosen ten goals for myself to work on. The first five of my goals deal with my spirituality, personal growth, relationships with my wife and children, and my health. Take a look at that list for a minute. You can see that by focusing first on myself and those who are most important to me, you can't help but keep life in balance. These are what I refer to as the relationship goals. The next five in my personal set of goals are the achievement goals. They cover a big item I would like to get, targets for my business to achieve, financial income, and books I want to see published.

By having ten goals to focus on, I personally am feeling less overwhelmed. And when I look back at my major accomplishments in life I can see that I was focused on only a few goals.

What about the rest of the 101 goals, you ask? Don't worry! Keep looking at your list as often as you can so you can *see* your goals. Just by seeing them over and over again you can never tell when a life change or opportunity will come your way that will make one of your other goals come immediately to the forefront.

Focus Points On Goals

Point #1: Three pieces of advice on achieving your goals. Write your goals down. Write your goals down. Write your goals down.

Point #2: Please read Point #1 again and do it. Don't even think of starting the next chapter before you write your goals down!

Point #3: By writing your goals down you have something you can read, visualize upon, and focus on, that helps you move beyond the little successes of those who do not write goals down.

Point #4: Begin with the end in mind. Work your way backwards from your goal to today's single step. Learn to live in the present and dream in the future.

Point #5: You have a lot of talents, characteristics, and skills that make you a success. Ask others to help you identify your strengths if you are having a hard time identifying them.

CHAPTER 8

CREATING YOUR FUTURE NOW!

Some people need to go beyond a year to have a stake in how the future unfolds. And for you, I will show you how to create your own Strategic Life Plan.

You have already identified your resources, you have a statement of purpose that keeps you pointed in the right direction, and you have examined your life with others over the next five years. And by now you should also have created your dream list of goals, all 101 of them.

Looking at your goals again, take a look at your long-range goals that you anticipated taking five years from today. Most people can get pretty overwhelmed thinking about setting five-year goals. And the typical step is to start with year one and cautiously move forward up to year five. That's not quite the way to achieve success the way you could. After all, you have so much potential.

What I am suggesting is you take a giant leap of faith, dream an IMAX theatre size image, and start right at year five where you absolutely long to be. When you do this, you will discover as I did, that you will be much further ahead than beginning at year one and progressing to year five.

Let me demonstrate what I mean. Money is a concrete example with which everyone can relate. Imagine you plan to increase this year's income by $5,000. The typical pattern of human nature would see each successive year thereafter probably limited to only a $1,000 increase. In five years your income would now be increased by $9,000.

Now let's have some fun with this and really focus on success. Project yourself to five years from today. You have to dream of yourself successfully working in the career of your dreams. You may ask of life anything you want. You are pre-pared to work towards this soon-to-be released goal. You boldly pronounce your dream of earning not $9,000 more a year but $25,000 by your fifth year.

For you to earn this much money you have to break your goal down into manageable chunks. This is where you can now work backwards from your ultimate destination. You could create a realistic target of earning $5,000 more each year for the preceding four years. So, going backwards with me, year four would have a goal of $20,000, year three of $15,000, year two would then have $10,000, with year one showing a goal to increase by $5,000.

Remember the usual way is to start with year one, plan to increase by $5,000 that year but be totally intimidated by your comfort zone to only increase by $1,000 for each successive year thereafter.

Interestingly, year one is the same for both approaches whether you start with year one or work your way backwards from year five. Yet the beauty of starting with year five is you have stretched yourself beyond your comfort zone. You have jumped forward into the future. You have risked only to dream. And you will see yourself achieve so much more when you make this giant leap of faith.

Balancing That Life Of Yours

Many people think of their goals only in the realm of money. While the reality is very true that we can't get along without it, make sure you understand the money goals illustrated above are only a concrete example that is bound to hit home for you. It's always amazing what a few dollar signs will do to grab someone's attention.

Yes, life is much more than just money. Remember success can be defined quite simply as the pursuit and achieving of any worthwhile goal or goals in life.

This is the reason why you were asked to draw up your life purpose before you wrote out your goals. When you start with goals, you are driven by tasks, by lists, by things. By focusing on your purpose and mission in life, if a goal ends up being unrealistic and unattainable, you will be driven to move on and work on another goal. Why? Because you won't be disappointed in having one goal not reached. You have a much higher cause propelling you to succeed, whatever that purpose may be for you.

Strategic Life Planning

When most organizations create a strategic plan, they look at which areas of service or products they need to focus on and then what are the operational goals they need to work on.

In a similar fashion, your Strategic Life Plan proposes eight areas within which to set goals. The first three focus on you: spiritual, mental, and physical development.

Spiritual—refers to looking at the meaning of life and where you fit in, and how you can draw on God or whatever perspective of a Higher Power you adhere to. This is the development of meditation and personal introspection and does not dictate going to a church or organized group, although that might be right for you.

Mental—looks at stimulating the mind and ensuring correct positive thinking. There is a wealth of good books to be read and courses to take, and personal and professional development. One can never stop learning or you will die, mentally.

Physical—is the obvious taking care of your body. You have a marvelous and unique human machine which you need to look after. You and I need to eat the right amount of healthy foods, exercise on a regular basis, and get sufficient rest.

The next two goal areas could be labeled as *relationship goals*, because they focus on family relationships and social relationships.

Family—life teaches you so much about yourself and the areas you need to improve. Developing a relationship with your spouse or partner should be foremost in your life. If you are blessed to have children they will definitely teach you a great deal about yourself. Goals like working on patience often become top of the list.

Socially—it is important to involve yourself with others, and especially with good friends. There is nothing like a get together with a few close friends to recharge the juices and have a good laugh over shared experiences.

The last two goal areas you can categorize as *achievement goals* as they look at your career development and financial plans.

Career—now more than ever, you have to plan ahead to keep your career. Do whatever you need to, in order to position yourself for the likely career changes in store for your future. If you are like me, you will have gone through a few career changes already. This makes it necessary to evaluate your skill-sets and talents on a regular basis and determine where you should be developing yourself.

Financially—you have to acquire a mind-set of prosperity consciousness which is first an attitude. Then you have to set in place a financial development plan and a future retirement plan. This may need some help from some financial planner friends but it's well worth the investment, no pun intended!

Community—with your focusing on yourself and your family, it is important to devote some time, money and energy towards others in your community. Whether this is business or professional associations, your church or faith community, service clubs, or just finding a need and volunteering your services. The bottom-line here is to give with no expectation of anything in return.

There is method to my madness in prioritizing the goal areas in the above order. You have to work on first things first. There has to be an inner balance before you can move outward and deal with other people and the tangible accomplishments you wish to achieve. You have to be on higher ground first before you can help someone else up. Then you can help others like family and friends who are more important than career and money. This order of priority should be compatible with your statement of purpose.

Stand Back And Look At Your Future

You have worked hard to get this far in the book. You should be commended for completing each of the exercises. And if you haven't done them yet, make time soon to do so and feel the exhilaration of having a plan.

Try to imagine having written out a five-year plan with absolutely no preparation ahead of time. It is doubtful you would have anything looking as good as what you will soon have written down on paper. You may never have even begun.

Furthermore, you would never have had a chance to first dream or to ask yourself what you want to achieve as a life purpose. Without a purpose to move you into action, goals rarely get achieved. Now you are ready.

STRATEGIC

	Year 5: _____ Age:	Year 4: _____ Age:
SPIRITUAL		
MENTAL		
PHYSICAL		
FAMILY		
SOCIAL		
CAREER		
FINANCIAL		
COMMUNITY		

LIFE PLANNING

Year 3: _____ Age:	Year 2: _____ Age:	Year 1: _____ Age:

Take a good, long look at the blank Strategic Life Plan on pages 124 and 125. Make copies of these pages to work from. Now look back at your 101 Goals List. Glance over the eight Strategic Life areas these goals will fall under. See that the first column is the year five column. You have just propelled yourself into the future! By starting with year five first, it will be easier to literally work your way backwards to year one.

Your job now is to write down the goals you see yourself achieving in year five for each area of your life. This is a leap of faith filled with exciting imagination to create what you've always wanted to be, to do, or to have. It's an expanded vision of the future through a wonderful and magical telescope.

The next task is to start shortening the telescope so you can see things a little bit closer. Here is where you have to create the goals you would have to be working on in year four, and then year three, all the way back to year one.

Let's follow the scene of a career goal of becoming an organizational psychologist, just as an example.

Your year five may have you completing your doctorate degree and starting employment at a leading corporation. In order for you to be there, your year four goal would have you in your second year of your Ph.D. program. In year three of your career goals, you would be in your first year of studies. Moving back to year two could have you doing a masters graduate program as well as year one.

Making It Happen

This was a course I began to follow because of my love of psychology and knowing what makes people tick. I was curious as to why organizations can be so volatile, or in contrast, so energizing.

I would have to get another masters degree, in psychology. Then I could proceed to start my doctorate.

My good wife told me I had her support as long as we did not borrow more funds and go further into debt. That is when I came up with the idea to get into professional speaking part-time to pay for my education. The funny thing is that I loved the speaking so much that my plans for getting a Ph.D. were scrapped.

Take the pursuit of the degree back to year one, and then go further back to this month, and on to this very week. Your action today may be as simple as phoning a university to send literature and calendars on their graduate programs in organizational psychology.

Imagine how you will feel when you get some mail that isn't junk mail, and it's addressed to you from a university. Don't you just get all kind of goosebumpy excited on the inside! It is so exhilarating to add another small step towards the journey of your goal five years from now.

While your career and education goal has a fairly fixed timetable, I have found that other less rigidly time bound goals will see themselves achieved ahead of schedule. Why? You have made the time to write them down. And there is magic in that action.

Second Verse, Same As The First

Now you do exactly the same thing for each of the eight areas identified in your Strategic Life Plan. For each area, you look through your telescope at year five and write down what it is you want to achieve. Then for each preceding year along that category, write down the goals you must reach that will help you achieve your year five objective.

It's also important to look back at your personal LifeLine. While things are being crafted on paper, examine each person's section and consider the events you want to see happening. Then it is just a matter of planning what you will do to make these activities happen. All ideas are welcome and need to be written as a goal under the appropriate category in the right year. Then you just keep stepping backwards to the smaller picture of today.

Your doctor may need to be consulted in case of shock or heart attack. But you now have before you, your very own draft version of a Strategic Life Plan.

All you have left to do now is to make it happen. And that requires some action.

The Final Plan...For Now!

Before revising your draft copy of your Strategic Life Plan, there are some important principles you need to consider in how you finally word your goals. Let's take a look at these guiding principles.

Principle 1   Use the present tense

When you write out your goals on your master copy, make sure they are in the present tense. There is an interesting thing that goes on in our minds when we do this. By writing it in the present tense you are using active verbs that will let your mind move you into action.

To just write your goals down in a stiff, objective manner, like "to lose weight", becomes so detached and lifeless that no wonder some people think goal setting never works. By adding the energizing form of the present tense of, *"I am at my ideal weight of..."* gives an automatic feeling of having achieved the goal. This creates an attitude of success even before you start to work on your goal.

Principle 2   Use positive language

You are probably so used to seeing life from a problem solving perspective, that it almost seems natural to write down your goals from a problem approach. So if you follow the losing weight example, you might think you should write down a goal like "I am losing ten pounds". After all, it is in the present tense.

This problem approach can create a problem by looking at your goal negatively. It's like asking someone not to think of a pink elephant. What do you first do when asked that? Of course! You think right away of a pink elephant. No matter how much you try to get it out of your mind.

Instead, write out your goal in words that focus on the *desired outcome*, which obviously makes it a positive. So our weight loss goal would change to " I weigh a hundred and forty-five pounds", or whatever the desired weight.

The neat thing about writing positive goals, is that every time you read and review your goals, you are reading them *as if* they were accomplished. This can't help but increase your *belief* power to see your goal through to completion.

Principle 3   Create plans of action

With your goals now written down in positive language and in the present tense, get them on to your master copy so you can photocopy it and carry it around with you.

Here is where a lot of people fall down. They write out their goals, especially at the end of a year or the very beginning of a new year. And that's where they stay, right there on paper.

You have to get into the habit of making daily action plans that will see you accomplish the goals you have set for yourself. This is going to take some self-discipline and regular reviews of the five year plan. From the five years you move down to this year, then quarterly check ups, monthly planning reviews, weekly actions, and daily specifics.

We'll talk more about this in the final *action packed* chapter. But first I want to share with you an experience that shows the power of writing down goals, even when you lose focus as I once did.

I am sure you will be able to relate to the situation. Your challenge will be in applying the principles in your own life. They are the key to your success.

I Want To Buy A House...With No Money!

For a long time I had written down the goal of buying our very first home. I had graduated with my masters degree when I was 30 years of age, resumed full-time employment once again, and had five children to feed and school loans to pay back to the bank.

It was going to take us 10 years to pay back our $30,000 student loans at the incredibly high interest rate of 13 1/2%. I graduated at the *wrong* time according to the economists. It seemed life was still very tight even when I was professionally employed.

The goal of purchasing a home began to fade for me personally, even though my wife faithfully looked at the real estate papers and sections in the newspaper. Irene takes care of the finances so she knew we had no money. Why was she still looking?

All of our friends and many much younger than I was, had their own homes. I was doing all the opposite things to what I have told you in this book.

First of all, I started to doubt. I was letting the seeds of doubt find a fertile place in my mind, rather that the seeds of faith. And there is an interesting fact about these two seeds. When you plant one the other can't grow at the same time. You literally have to pull the one out if you want the other one to find room to grow.

I was also allowing a whole negative attitude to creep right on in and fill up my mind with *what if* scenarios from the past. I even started to get a little jealous of those who had their own homes.

With a lacking in belief and a definite wrong attitude I put my goal away of having our own home.

Then motivational and business speaker, Brian Tracy, came to our city giving a presentation on *The Psychology of Success*. Attending this got me all pumped up again. The juice of enthusiasm, excitement and energy was rekindled and raring to go.

Brian had us write down a question or "problem", a challenge as he preferred to have us call it, at the top of a piece of paper. Then we were to brainstorm 20 ideas on how to reach that goal or solve that challenge.

The challenge that I wrote down was "how to buy a detached four bedroom home with no money".

As he explained to us that night, the first five ideas would be quite easy. From 5 to 10 we probably thought quite highly of ourselves for the brilliance of our thinking. But the last 10 would stretch every facet of our brain cells. Furthermore, we could not stop until all 20 ideas were written down! That was painful. And my list saw unusual statements like "finding 100 people to each give us $1,000". I wish!

Remember you can't be critical of any of your ideas, no matter how crazy or far fetched they may seem.

Once you have your list, the idea is to prioritize your suggestions and just go through the list one by one until you strike gold.

For your benefit, on pages 132 and 133 are a couple of work sheets to help you *mindstorm* a solution to your major goal or current challenge.

And so that is exactly what I did. Except for one minor detail. I hid that piece of paper away in my briefcase. Would you believe I let it sit there? Why? In hindsight, I think I was still so full of doubt that even all the wonderful motivational ideas that came from Brian Tracy's seminar could not take root until I sowed the seed of belief.

Learning To Weed Out Doubt

While my wife and I had told each other we would give up looking at house ads, she began to look again. You see you cannot put a doubt seed in to someone who has a belief seed already growing. Irene strongly believed and even *felt* we would find a house to buy in the near future.

Knowing how I had been feeling about house hunting, she cautiously approached me when there was a semi-detached, three bedroom house available on a street where some friends of ours lived. With a smile on her face and a hopeful gleam in her eye, she asked if we could go and look at it that weekend.

It was then that I pulled my piece of paper out of my briefcase with 20 solutions on how to buy the house of our dreams without any money. My wife looked at me with complete surprise that I had even been thinking about buying a house. Naturally, she was super excited that now both of us were entertaining the idea of getting a house.

So with the help of my wife's enthusiasm and belief, and the mindstorming sheet that gave some potential, if not crazy ideas (thanks to Brian Tracy), I finally pulled out that plant called doubt and sowed a new seed of *belief*. It was going to germinate and grow very fast in the next two weeks, as you'll soon see.

The next thing was to go beyond thinking and to see this house for ourselves. It was a great starter home and was already vacant as the owners had transferred to Ottawa. There was all the potential to make it work for our family, while knowing it was much smaller than we needed. The bottom-line was we liked it. It *felt* right.

So we went over to our friends on the same street and told them about the house. They told us to put an offer in for it, to which we both cracked up laughing. "But we don't have any money!" "Put an offer in anyway," was their simple response. That's when we called our real estate friend.

The House That Faith Bought

Our real estate friend met with us and supported the idea of at least putting an offer in. Nothing ventured, nothing gained.

Now write down your goal or challenge that you want to succeed at. Brainstorm the ideas to reach it, and don't quit until you have 20 ideas written down. Then follow through with the rest of the steps listed. Make your dream happen!

MINDSTORMING ACTION PLANNER

1. Rewrite the goal or challenge you wish to generate some ideas for.

Goal:_____

_____

2. Now, personally brainstorm 20 ideas for reaching your goal. Do not judge any idea when writing it down. The first five to ten ideas will seem easy to generate. The last ten will require all your creative juices, craziness and attention

1._____

2._____

3._____

4._____

5._____

6._____

7._____

8._____

9._____

10._____

MINDSTORMING ACTION PLANNER
(Continued)

11._____

12._____

13._____

14._____

15._____

16._____

17._____

18._____

19._____

20._____

3. Evaluate and revise actions as needed. Prioritize the top five ideas you feel willing to tackle by placing a circle around the idea number, and by putting a rank order number beside the circled number.

4. For one of the circled ideas, ideally your top ranked, write down the steps you will take to make this idea work. Do the same for each idea as needed.

Step 1 _____

Step 2 _____

Step 3 _____

Step 4 _____

Step 5 _____

5. Transfer your steps to your Daily Planner and go to it and make each step happen towards your ideas.

With the opportunity we had to see the house, it was that much easier to *visualize* it and focus on *believing* we would get it. So an offer was submitted that was low. The sellers saw this as an insult and counter-offered high. We came up a notch from where we had been, and the next thing we know they had accepted!

Now, we had fourteen days to come up with over a hundred thousand dollars. There is nothing like a good challenge to get creativity surging, and that's when I pulled out my sheet of paper with the 20 ideas.

The first idea was to ask family or friends for the down payment as a loan. I clearly remember praying as specifically as I have ever done, and offering to use this home to benefit others in any way we could. The person we had identified was asked and responded with a request for time to think about it. Talk about a tense moment when we had to stay *focused* on *believing* and maintaining a positive *attitude*.

Within a few days we received an affirmative answer. All we had to do now was get a mortgage and we would be all set. Or so we thought.

Apparently, the financial laws do not allow you to borrow 100% of the funding to buy a house. We knew we could handle it but there was no one we could convince otherwise.

Then came the grand test. A few banks would give us a partial mortgage if we would sign a particular form. The form simply stated the down payment we had received was a gift and had no terms of repayment. Based on our values it was a quick and simple reply. No! It wasn't honest. We were told everyone does it. We were not "everyone"!

We went down the 20 ideas list with no success. Our mortgage broker soon realized we were prepared to lose the house rather than compromise our values. That decision stirred him to call around all the banks and trust companies just one more time.

It was on this last round that one lone trust company agreed to give us a partial mortgage if we would give them a photocopy of the down payment cheque and of our bank balance. That was no problem. We had the cheque, and our bank balance was zero!

Our next job was to come up with $12,500, the remaining amount needed to buy our house.

We tried out second mortgages but the rate of interest was in the high teens and we knew we could not afford that. Having obtained in such a miraculous way the bulk of the money, the difference seemed so much easier to believe that we would really get it.

But there was no doubt it was the hardest to get. We learned to ask a lot of people for wild and woolly ideas to generate the capital we needed. We were just three days away from the close of the offer. What were we to do?

Not once did we doubt. After all it was our house, and we had over 80% of the money for it. We had to re-focus.

Never, Never, Never Give Up!

Then with one day to spare, our real estate agent came to us and wanted to talk. He asked if we had come up with anything. At that point it was quite easy for us to confidently reply with, *"not yet!"*. We firmly believed something was going to happen. And it did.

Our real estate agent told us that he saw our family as honest and hard working. He could see our faith and determination. And then he shared with us that he had been to his own bank that day to find out how much the rate of interest would be for the amount of money we needed. He openly told us he had only done this once before in his life, that this was not something he did for everyone. You guessed it. He had borrowed the difference and gave it to us as a second mortgage at a rate of interest we could afford.

So within fourteen days we had bought a house with no money of our own.

Who said miracles still don't happen?

Remember to always keep your goals written down. My goal had been for a detached four-bedroom home, and this house didn't fit that criteria.

Within three years interest rates came down and we were able to buy up into a detached *five* bedroom, four level back split home. So we even gained a bedroom on top of what I had wished for. The brainstormed ideas helped us get our first house. The goal I wrote down with the specific description became the focus point to continually look towards. Having this focused goal helped us get the house we really wanted.

So never look down upon the stepping stones of lesser accomplishments like our first house. It was still a miracle. And we eventually leveraged its worth to purchase our present home. Don't ever give up on your goals!!

Focus Points On Goals

Point #1: Live life with a purpose. By creating your very own purpose statement it will help you to always focus your energy, time and resources on achieving your goals.

Point #2: Plan some of your goals around your LifeLine so you can capture the wonderful events of those who are most important to you.

Point #3: Make room in your life to write out all 101+ goals. Attempt to write as many down as you can at one time. Then come back and keep adding. Let yourself go and write down everything you ever wanted to be, things you want to have, and things to do.

Point #4: Count the cost, provide a plan, and advance with action. Evaluate your goals and see what is necessary to make them happen.

Point #5: Success is having achieved a balanced life. Do it!

RELATIONSHIPS COME FIRST

As I reviewed this book to this point I realized that some people could still think that success was purely a materialistic objective, especially because of the many tangible and financial examples I have shared with you so far.

While I let my mind wander on this matter, I recalled a vintage film piece from comedians Abbott and Costello. This was called "Who's on first, and what's on second" and had a baseball game as the context for this very funny skit. It's worth renting if you haven't seen it before.

The title of this comic routine helped me see that I had to write a chapter on relationships. How on earth did I get that connection? Look again. It's *"who's* on first", that is *people* must come first. And it's *"what's* on second", which implies that *things* are second.

In focusing on relationships as a key to success, you need to put aside any personal and selfish interests. One of my daughters was with me when we saw a van in a parking lot at our downtown library. It had a vanity license plate that read "EGO". I told her that just like that van, we have to leave our egos in the parking lot.

Building relationships is not a 50/50 thing of just giving to get. It is giving 110% all the time with no expectation in return. However, as sure as night is followed by day, your actions will be the seeds sown that will be harvested with dividends at some time in the future. The Law of the Harvest will always prevail.

Keeping A People First Priority

By putting people ahead of things, you are moving in the right direction for keeping a healthy balance while pursuing whatever focus of success you have chosen.

I met with millionaire Ben Kubassek, author of the recently published book *Success Without Burnout*. In this enlightening book, Ben shares from his own personal experience the price one can pay for success if you are not balanced in all areas of your life. He tells of his near nervous breakdown as he reached the burnout point from being a workaholic. He knows now that he was setting goals and kept raising the bar because he was never satisfied. Never was there time set aside to refuel himself.

The price he finally paid was with his health; physically, mentally, emotionally and spiritually. Outside of himself, the so-called success he had achieved had seriously affected the relationships with his wife and children, extended family, and co-workers.

He reviews in his book some of the tried and true methods, as well as some of his own farm-rooted wisdom for handling stress and burnout. He speaks to people at a personal, family and business level on how to re-focus their lives by balancing the many facets of life. Putting relationships first is the key.

What if....?

We have probably all been in some course or class where a teacher or presenter has asked you to imagine what you would do if you only had a year to live. Then they keep giving you less time, like six months and ask you what you would do. Finally, they get you down to just one day to live. Almost to a person, as the time gets less and less, people focus on wanting to be around the ones they love and care for. Relationships are so important.

It really is interesting how your mind becomes attracted to articles, stories, and observations that relate to what you speak or want to write about. While thinking on the topic of relationships, I came across this quote used by a closing speaker at a university commencement address. The quote was from a Dr. Bernadine Healy, who said:

> *"As a physician who has been deeply privileged to share the most profound moment's of people's lives, including their final moments, let me tell you a secret. People facing death don't think about degrees they have earned, what positions they have held, or how much wealth they have accumulated. At the end, what really matters is who you loved and who loved you. The circle of love is everything and is a good measure of a past life. It is the gift of greatest worth."*

I like that; the circle of love is the gift of greatest worth. The circle of love is the outreached arms and the connection of relationships.

Now try imagining that one of your closest family members or friends is going to die tomorrow. They don't know they are going to die, but you have been privileged to know this so you can make their last day a very special one. Wouldn't you treat them a lot differently? Wouldn't some of the tasks we deem so important lose all sense of priority compared with the value of the relationship you want to build while there is still time? Wouldn't you rather give them flowers while they are alive? Yes, so many things would change. Life would be treasured. Relationships would be revered.

Top Of The List

When I ask people to prioritize the relationships in their life, it is amazing how difficult this is for many. Some folks have created such a dependency and controlling attitude towards the special people in their lives, they never make time for themselves or any higher cause or relationships.

In my presentations, I suggest people should first have down a relationship with God, or a belief in a Higher Power. If not, they should at least have a guiding set of life values. A spiritual relationship can be a source of enriching comfort, solace, and direction in times of need. It allows you to express supreme gratitude and thanksgiving for the wonderful blessings you have received. Truly, you should count all of your blessings you have received and realize how much God, or whatever Higher Power you recognize, has done for you.

It is important to make time for meditation, studying of scriptures, reading of inspirational books, prayer and solitude to reflect. During these times of spiritual introspection will often come the answers to your challenges.

Being able to worship with others who share your beliefs, and serve others is so important in the fellowship of those who live in your community. Affiliate yourself with a church, synagogue, or organization you feel brings truth and meaning to your life.

When you have been given so much from God, family, friends and sometimes complete strangers, it is important to give something back in return as the very least you can do. Give of your time and your means. Share your talents with others to help them become successful in life.

10 Cents On The Dollar

The principle of the tithe taught in the Bible and many other inspired writings, is another universal law of thanksgiving and a profound spiritual principle. Each of us have been given health, strength, intellect, talents and abilities to earn what we can for ourselves and give what we can to others. Some see the giving of a tenth of one's income as a sacrifice. To give back just one tenth to our church and to our community is merely a token of gratitude and not a sacrifice.

Children have a such a simple understanding of the Law of Tithing. If you gave them ten apples and then asked for just one back, they would readily give you one and more than likely want to give you two or three! Somehow, when we get to be adults, that selfish streak we have acquired has us thinking it's all ours.

Some of the best speakers in the business are known to freely give a tenth of their speaking business away to non-profit organizations, as just one way of giving something back to their communities for all they have been blessed with.

Not only does giving a tithe of all that you receive help you to realize the incredible blessings you have received in life, but you end up being able to bless others as well. It teaches us selflessness and goes a long way to help us learn to budget wisely.

There is also an incredible promise the Bible gives us for all those who pay tithing. It says if you pay a tithe you will be so blessed in return you won't have room enough for all the blessings God will pour out upon you (Malachi 3:8-12). This miraculous blessing not only refers to prosperity but also to peace of mind. Most people struggle to obtain the peace of mind they desire. All they have to do is give of themselves in order to find themselves.

Peace of mind is a natural by-product of seeking out true success. Paying a tithe can only help you in your search. It will also help you learn to mange your money to be successful.

Following Your Values

If you do not hold to a particular religious faith, then it is important to at least identify the life values that you hold to be fundamental to your personal beliefs. By writing out your values you are able to see what it is you stand for, what is important to you, and what makes you tick.

Even reflecting on your values will cause you to think about how you should be living, and how that will impact those around you. None of us live in isolation. You have to make sure that living your values is not in violation of the spiritual or value based philosophy of another individual.

Living up to a higher ideal flows naturally into the reason for having an overriding purpose that governs your personal, family and business life. As you have seen in making your goals, that guiding purpose statement and the foundation of your set of values, you cannot fail to find greater happiness in the balance of reaching your goals.

Value Added Life

There are many viewpoints on how to generate your values. Some suggest creating values for each of the roles you live, or for each major goal areas you have written down. I have personally been overwhelmed by the multiplicity of values many of these people will suggest. It can become complicated. I found too many values caused me to lose focus.

You may find as I have, that having a small, comprehensive set of values is all you really need. Five has been a comfortable number that has worked for me, and I have seen other authors and speakers use the same number.

These values follow along with your purpose statement and further help you to focus on your goals. They also help you with your decision making by being able to see whether a decision fits with your values.

For my personal set of values I wrote down the things in my life that meant the most to me. Then I rank ordered them as best as I could. It was an interesting exercise and took me a while before I completed it to my liking.

My five values, in the order of priority, are as follows:

1. *My faith in God is foremost.*
2. *Relationships with my family come first.*
3. *Helping others to achieve and personally make a difference.*
4. *Live with integrity, respect others, and recognize everyone's efforts.*
5. *Bring joy to others and personally enjoy life.*

I have been able to boil these simple phrases down to five words that again help me to focus on my values: *faith; family; helping; integrity; joy.* In a very concrete way I can associate them with the fingers on one hand and never forget them.

While I will not profess to be perfect at living these values, they certainly help me to remember what is important in my life and re-direct energies that could have gone elsewhere. They help me to re-*focus.*

Try it yourself. Write down your first attempt at figuring out your top five values in life with short phrases. It's the old story of getting it down first and rewriting them later.

My Five Values

1. _____

2. _____

3. _____

4. _____

5. _____

Now that you have written your values out in basic phrase form, see if you can further simplify them and boil them down to some core words that will help you to consistently remember them. Try to prioritize them according to importance of relationships and strength of values.

My Five Core Value Words

    1. _____
    2. _____
    3. _____
    4. _____
    5. _____

Next On The List Is...

You of course! After your spiritual focus on God or a set of values to live by, you need to make sure that your goals truly do allow you to be balanced. You need to have plenty of opportunities to recharge yourself spiritually, physically, mentally and emotionally. If you are going to make a difference in this great, big, beautiful world, you are going to have to be on higher ground first before you can ever help someone else and pull them up.

When Jesus Christ spoke of the greatest commandments, the first was to love God. The second was like the first, and stated you had to love others in the same way as you love yourself (see Luke 10:27). Many of the worlds religions speak of similar teachings of loving each other. Now this is not a narcissistic, egotistical love. This is the love we have referred to elsewhere in this book, of remembering your great worth and potential. We must remove the labels and put downs we have stored in our minds. We have to repeatedly tell ourselves over and over again, that we are special.

Once you are able to focus on your worth, you should be able to see what self-esteem expert and author Jack Canfield would say, that you are *lovable* and *capable*. When you can fully accept this, you will begin to fully grow. When you can begin to unlearn anything that has been taught you contrary to this belief, your life will begin to soar.

Review your goals frequently so you can make sure you are covering all the bases that will put you "on first".

Make sure you are taking time out for yourself spiritually, physically, mentally, socially and emotionally. By putting *you* first after your spiritual relationship with God, or your own set of values and beliefs, you will see that you are in much better shape to deal with the next set of relationships.

Focus Points on Relationships

Point #1: Always remember the Abbott and Costello skit *Who's On First*, to recall that people come before material possessions.

Point #2: Live each day as if it were your last. Treat each person as if it were their last day.

Point #3: No matter what your faith, beliefs or values, having something greater than you to believe in, should keep you focused on what is most important in life.

Point #4: When you focus on helping people, somehow happiness and success seem naturally attracted to you. Find someone who needs your help today.

Point #5: Give something back for all you have been blessed with. Whether this is your church, community, neighbourhood or for a local charity, follow the principle of the tithe.

CHAPTER 10

VERY IMPORTANT PEOPLE

Many people will pick up this book and think as I did when I first got into motivational, self-help books. Some will think that success is purely striving for material and monetary gain. This is where the Biblical notion of "money is the root of all evil" leads to a very negative perception behind the word *success*. Careful review of this quote indicates clearly that it is not money that is the root of all evil, but the *love of money* that causes the problems.

One way to take care of this perception problem is to make certain you love people and not things.

I like the following quote spoken by the late David O. McKay, to help us truly focus on what is most important in life:

No success can compensate for failure in the home.

Now *there* is something to reflect on when you get out of focus and balance with goals that are too much on achieving and not enough on relationships. The result is sacrificing those who are most important to you for some*thing*. By focusing on your family after yourself, you are putting the most important things, or rather people, in your life first.

The amazing part is as you do this, all the other things in your life seem to fall into place. Well, I guess they don't *fall* into place. You *put* them in place by prioritizing your spouse and children at the top of your life. You will see yourself constantly fed by love and friendship, memories and feelings. All of this far exceeds any tangible accomplishment or position in society.

Too Great A Price

In some of my community and church volunteer work, I have come across men and women who sacrifice marriages and family for material things. For some, success was working too many hours with plenty of reasons given as to why, and with the classic response of "only wanting to provide for the family". Others have turned to the bottle of alcoholism, and yet others have become "drunken" with the glory of position and fame in the company, only to forget about the position and fame of being a husband or wife, and mother or father at home. Some resort to abuse in an attempt to secure a position of control, only to lower themselves to the very dust in the eyes of those who should love them the most.

We must learn from the number of broken marriages and destroyed families around us. We must see our spouse and children as the most important people in our lives. Then, perhaps, other's failure will have been a useful teacher. The key behind this failure is to learn from others around you and not to experience it yourself. Scars run too deep in the lives of those affected and the battlefield of broken homes carry too many tragedies.

Being A Best Friend
Every Single Day

But there are plenty of simple solutions to keep your marriage alive and well, and your family and home as happy and peaceful as relationships can allow.

Let's first deal with our spouse and we'll talk about children in a little while.

You have to look back to the first time you met each other. There was usually some fun activity going on, or maybe you were at the same school, work or community and just plain knew each other. Those first fleeting glances; the smiles at one another; the twinkle in your eyes; the conversations that never seemed to end; and the genuine caring and concern for one another; all built something unique. You discovered that you were becoming more than just friends. You were the *best of friends* each and every day.

The great secret to keeping a marriage relationship alive is to *continue* to be the best of friends. Best friends take time out to do special things. They seem to inherently know what the other person is thinking or going to say. For those of you with a positive relationship with a partner, you will relate with the occurrence of often thinking the same thing as the other at the same time. Or you just think alike on so many things.

A best friend is able to bite their tongue on the little things that irk others, and tries hard to find a way to tell you about the big things so you don't hurt others or each other. Somehow a best friend is always there to listen.

Little Things Are Always
Big Things

There is one thing you may have discovered as I have, that in marriage it is little things that cause big problems, and it is little things that make a big difference.

Take communication as an example. It seems the number one problem in most marriage relationships is poor communication. Money matters and sexual intimacy follow close behind. Yet, lack of communication is the most common issue and ironically lies ahead of the other two weak spots of finances and sex.

My wife, Irene, feared that we would run out of things to talk about when we were newly married. Now, after 18 years as husband and wife, there are many nights where we have to convince each other to stop talking and go to bed!

The Greatest Investment

All relationships require you to make an important investment. The first thing you have to give is your time.

Even this evening before I started writing this, I can see that I invested time to help do the dishes. I spent some time with my two boys to enjoy a half-hour children's TV show together. Then some more time was put into reading some bedtime stories to my youngest child. And later on I spent a fair time with my oldest boy getting stumped by a simple mathematics question. The return on my investment was some laughter over the math, an enjoyable story, a TV show with a message to live by, and an overall good feeling inside.

You also have to pay a few other things. Like paying attention. You really have to put all your energy and focus into the person with whom you are investing time, and the rest of your life.

Sometimes you have to stop your own thoughts midstream and say *"stop!"*, just so you can focus on the person you're with. Put all of your other interests aside and put your family member right in front.

The only measure your children may ever have that they mean something to you, is in the time you invest in them. We must never lull ourselves into a false sense of security by just giving *quality* time. It must also be *quantity* time.

Keeping A Regular Date

I didn't have the greatest opportunity to do a lot of courting before we got married, so I sometimes feel under-privileged as far as the romancing experience. But one thing we have maintained over our married years, even during our student years together, is having a weekly date.

In those frugal, student years, our dates were mostly playing board games or going window shopping. When we saved up enough money to really splurge, we would go to the local Ponderosa restaurant in our area. We would sit by the salad bar just to people-watch how folks would load up their salad plate. We got pretty good at predicting how people would behave just by first impressions. What can I say? It was a cheap date!

One of the things we do now is to alternate between each of us in planning what our fun activity will be. While we occasionally watch a classic movie, you should strive to have a date that will permit you to communicate with one another. Don't hide behind a movie or TV show. Remember to *spend* time together and get to know more about each other. You'll be amazed as you stumble upon little known items from your spouse's past, or just discover more about each other. This is building relationships.

Time With Mom And Dad

Children also need one-on-one time with each of their parents, if the family dynamics allow this opportunity. We try to go out with each child once a month, unevenly divided between the two of us. This does not always work out and we remind each other of the need to schedule these moments in.

These activities can be simple things, but oh so big in the eyes of your children. Sometimes I think it doesn't even matter what the activity is in the eyes of the child. It's that opportunity to have the one-on-one time to talk and be together with you.

Recent activities have been going to a *Star Trek* event and watching a movie; getting some silver coins appraised; redeeming Hallowe'en coupons for an ice cream treat; going to a restaurant and having the child order for both of you; skating at the local arena; going for a drive together while on a business errand; accompanying a visit to an 80 year old lady's birthday party; going to an art gallery or children's museum; and the list continues.

Each of these events are cemented into the minds of our children and our own minds, by time, experiences, memories, short and long talks, and putting your children first.

One last point. When the children were young they all referred to these activities as dates. As the boys got older they preferred to call them "outings". But they still want them, whatever you call them.

Weekly Family Time

This title is misleading because I do not suggest you only see your family once a week. But we all know that with the busy schedules of children and parents alike, homework, sports, cubs, scouts, guides, youth nights, dances, association, church, and business meetings, can all get in the way of everyone being home at the same time.

So one night a week we take time out together. The TV stays off and the phone is left to the answering machine, and each of us takes turns planning what we are going to do. With five children and two adults, the sky is the limit as to the creativity of ideas that come up.

This has ranged from playing some of our many board games; playing soccer by blowing through straws at ping-pong balls on the kitchen table; acting out charades; drawing win/lose/or draw charades; roasting marshmallows on a fire at a nearby park; visiting the library all together; making all kinds of good food treats, with some being given away; visiting family members; going canoeing and finding out your children are better than you are; having a talent show; making crafts; acting out stories with dress-up clothes; attending sports events; and you name it and we've probably come close to doing it.

Our most exotic family night was when my wife gave her father a hot-air balloon ride for both of them to celebrate his eightieth birthday. Our family came armed with cameras and video-recorder, and we followed in hot pursuit with goodies and drinks in our van.

The bottom-line is to spend as much *time* (there's that word again) as you and circumstances permit you to have together. And remember to have a camera on hand to make your memories last.

Making Traditions

Another thing you can do to instill life and love into your family relationships, is to create traditions.

Every time Christmas approaches we enjoy our traditions of making gingerbread men (and women) advent calendars that we give away to neighbours and friends, putting up the Christmas tree with music playing, making gingerbread houses to give to teachers and special people, and closer to Christmas day going out carol singing to our neighbours bearing cookies on wrapped Styrofoam trays.

Each year as we begin the annual traditions, there is a linking of relationships. We relive the past and share recalled experiences as we form new memories to add to this year's living of our traditions.

No matter what your culture, race, or religion, it is your traditions that help cement the relationships between each generation. Often we can take our traditions for granted. Make time to write down your traditions so that your children can take some of them into their own families.

If You Love 'Em, Tell 'Em

This is something I have personally had to learn to do, and I still have to remind myself to keep telling my children I love them. In my home growing up as a child, I didn't hear the words "I love you". My wife, Irene, helps me to stay on my toes by asking me if I have recently spoken those essential words to each child.

You know you love them. But if you don't tell them, your children will assume the opposite. Also, don't just tell them when you are saying good-night to them. No problem saying it at bedtime. It's just that it can become too routine. So make sure you catch those special moments elsewhere at different times to tell them. Like on a date or outing.

Say It From The Roof Tops

I remember when we lived in this one house. When the children walked to their bus stop, we could open up our bedroom window and the screen and shout out, *"Good-bye! I love you!"* The neat thing was that when the children would get to this certain gap between houses they would look our way, wave, and yell back the same words.

One day my oldest daughter had to stay home from school for some reason, and it was my turn to walk along the same route the children did each morning. Caught up in my own world while walking along, at this certain point along the way I distinctly heard the words lofting through the air, *"Good-bye, Dad! I love you!"* I suddenly realized I was not hearing voices. I turned and found myself looking through this gap between the houses to see my daughter waving at me from the bedroom window. Completely oblivious to those around me, and caught up in the thrill of hearing my daughter expressing her affection, I waved back vigorously and yelled at the top of my voice, *"I love you too!"*

I remember chuckling to myself, wondering what the people walking along that sidewalk were thinking to themselves. Especially if they hadn't heard my daughter's initial greeting. Was I crazy or something? But just like the retelling of this experience, the feelings and memories of that day come vividly back for me to share it with you. I will never forget that day yelling back to my daughter that I loved her.

Taking Care of Business

One of the neat things about having your own business is that you learn very quickly to focus on your clients or customers.

As I have researched what clients and customers want most from businesses, the overwhelming response is the desire for a personal relationship with the service or sales people. They want to be considered more than just a number. Get to know them and keep a record of their family members, likes and dislikes, special dates and conversations. With many of the contact management systems on computer, this is much easier to do. But the old standby of a notebook or index cards works just fine as well.

Clients say they want you to call just to find out how they are with no business on your agenda. When you send them a card at birthdays and holidays, they are tired of the impersonalized signature. Take the time to write a little note that shows you were thinking of them, and not just the business opportunities.

Create and send a newsletter to your clients. Even if you only photocopy articles of other people's newsletters, and highlight them all up showing points you think would benefit your clients, it shows you care.

And lastly, remember what your mother taught you long ago to always say "thank you". Believe it or not, many of the individuals I have surveyed say that they rarely get a word of thanks after a business transaction or sale. So take the time to show, write and say your thank you's for the business you get.

When In Doubt

There are many times that I get asked a question about dealing with employees or clients that I have never encountered before. At first you think, *"Oh cute! How do I answer this one?"*. Then a recollection of some family experience will come into my mind. With five children this is easier than you may think. Time and time again, the solution is building relationships through more communication, more time, and more expression of showing that you care. Even that you love them.

One Big Happy Family

So remember. From the top of your relationship list to the bottom of your list, the solutions are always the same. Treat everyone as family, as if you were at home even when at work. Then you will be certain to be focusing on real success!

Focus Points on Relationships

Point #1: Plan to have a weekly date with your spouse and bring back the fun. Courtship doesn't have to end at the altar.

Point #2: Take time to sharpen your saw if you ever want to *cut* it in life. Keep a balance of your physical, mental, emotional, social and spiritual areas of your life.

Point #3: Put your family ahead of any other success, and the other success will seek you out.

Point #4: It really is the little things that count. Do something special today for one of the special people in your life.

Point #5: If you're not used to it, take a risk, open up your heart and give a family member a big hug and tell them you love them. Next time you do this, notice how you feel inside.

Point #6: Taking care of your business is really building relationships. If you build the relationships, the business will come. And when you don't know what to do for a client, treating them like family always works wonders.

CHAPTER 11

MOVING INTO ACTION!

This is where everything you have read so far, all the things you have written down on paper, all the desires and passion that you have drummed up....this is where all of this comes to the reality of *action.*

You have been doing some fairly passive action by just reading this book. Some of you will just read the book and not carry out the suggested activities that will help you truly focus on success. Others need to read through the book first to catch the big picture, and then will go back and complete the exercises. Either way, plan to take action today! Make this the time where you actually make your success happen. No one else is going to do it for you.

Some people will complete the activities of identifying their life purpose and even getting all their goals written down in a Strategic Life Plan. And that's where it stays. On paper only.

If it's any help to you, I know. I have not only been there, done that, I continue to fight the easy way out to make my goals get off the paper and come alive.

In driving around you often see those great quotes that are displayed on portable signs outside businesses and churches. One that I saw just recently hits the nail on the head for this chapter. It simply stated, *"the secret of action is to begin!"*. So let's begin.

Reviewing The Journey Of Success

You have definitely come a long way to have read this far into this book. Many people quit after the second chapter and either add the book to their bookshelves or return it the library or friend they borrowed it from.

So for you who have wanted to make your journey to success a reality, let's review what we set out to do.

The first focus we talked about was believing that you can succeed. You need to create a burning desire in your heart, soul, and mind that you will achieve that which is most important to you.

This belief has to get to the point where you can *see* your goal in your mind's eye. You must drive this belief deep into your subconscious as well as your conscious mind. Even when we discussed belief earlier, we learned how this incredible force of just believing can motivate us towards acting out certain behaviours that would lead us to succeed.

Your belief has to become stronger and stronger so you can discover for yourself that you *feel* your belief as well as see, hear, smell and touch it. And this feeling is on the inside and not the outside.

Finally, as we concluded the focusing on belief you were strongly encouraged to believe in your dreams. Make your dreams come true by *doing* something each and every day to keep the dream alive.

So What Do You Believe?

As I shared with you in the beginning of this book, I have had to ask this question of myself several times in my life. At no time has this been more important to me than right now.

By venturing into my own business as a professional speaker and consultant, I *must* believe that I have a message important enough to share that I would be willing to do it for free. I have to *love* what I do and not just *like* it. There are only two letters that are different between the words "love" and "like", but that little difference is a *big* difference.

Try getting away with only telling your spouse that you *like* him or her for a whole month. Then tell me if there is a difference between "like" and "love" or not!

This is where the problem starts. People write down their goals and they are only in *like* with their goals and dreams. And just as liking someone will never get you to the wedding altar, neither will liking a goal or dream make it come about.

Right now, my *belief* in what I am doing and what I want to do with my life is enabling me to write this book. Why? Because I believe in what I have written, and I believe you can benefit from that belief and what I have experienced in my life. See what belief can do!

Creating A Whole New Attitude

You will probably recall that while belief is the foundation for success, you need to develop a constant positive attitude focused on achieving success.

Getting the right kind of attitude requires that you get rid of the wrong kind of attitudes. You have to create a mental position in your mind that is positive, energizing, and motivating for you to be able to achieve whatever you want to have, be, or do.

This means you have to remove any *doubt* from your mind. You cannot even begin to entertain the idea of failure. And even if a failure does show up (and trust me they do come along), you will be able to see them as something to learn from and move on to success.

Another attitude to exercise is that you and I create our own *fears*. Sometimes these fears are passed on to us from family and friends, but remember, fears are a *learned* experience. The solution to all our fears, no matter what they are or how long you have had them, is that fears can be *unlearned*.

This is going to take *action* on your part to learn whatever new skills and behaviours that will help eradicate once and for all the fears holding you back. So if it's true that you and I create our own fears, then that means that it is *you* and *I* that hold ourselves back from succeeding in life.

Develop the belief and attitudes in your self to *risk* stepping out of your comfort zone and to " boldly go where no man (or woman!) has gone before!"

The key to focusing on attitude is feeding the mind. Feed the mind with nutritious, rich and rewarding thoughts. Fuel the heart with inspiring and invigorating quotes from successful people, both past and present. Collect posters and plaques to fill your home and office with the positive images and words you want to fill your mind.

So Where Are You At?

What have you been doing to fill your mind with the positive, uplifting attitudes that will propel you towards the success you dream about? Are you removing the negativity of lousy TV shows and movies that will sap you dry? Are you taking the time to read books that leave you recharged? What about listening to or watching audio- and videotapes of motivational speakers, or autobiographies of people you can look up to?

Do you have a list of motivating quotes that mean a lot to you? If not, take the time to write down your favourite ones.

Print them up in large print and plaster them around your room where you work.

It is so true, that without working on your *attitude* you will never raise your *altitude* towards success.

Putting Life In Focus

Have you noticed any trend in the review steps we are looking at? In order to really make it in life and succeed, all of the focus points we have looked at together require you to take lots of *action* steps.

Notice how each of the focus areas examined moves progressively from the intangible to the tangible? *Belief* is the least tangible and requires the most effort to generate the power behind this concept. *Attitudes* is another exercise in mind development but at least you can draw on words and images to leave their imprint on the mind, heart and soul.

The next area we looked at was focus. To *focus* on focusing was likened to a camera. You may be able to see what you want in life through the lens of a camera. But unless you focus your lens, you will never be able to see the object of your desires with any clarity.

It is having a *clear vision* of what it is you really want to have, or the career or position you want to be, or just the things you have always wanted to do, that will *see* things begin to happen.

This is where you were taught how to use the incredible results that can be achieved from *visualization*. Visualization draws on such powerful classics as Napoleon Hill's book *Think and Grow Rich,* with that memorable affirmation *"whatever the mind of man can conceive and believe it can achieve."* In other words, you have to see it to believe it and this is perfectly fine in your imagination first.

You were told to use all the senses available to you to generate an intense, indelible image that is permanently etched in your mind.

Another suggestion was to move closer to the tangible side of making success a reality by making a *dream book*. This can be with either the actual pictures of something you want, or a whole collage of pictures from all of your goals.

Can You Really See It?

That is the question I have to ask myself constantly. Can I really see what it is I want to achieve? Can you see yourself moving towards your goals and actually achieving something you only dreamed of being able to reach? If you can, you should give yourself a gold star and pat yourself on the back. If this is an area that you find tough, it's because it is and you are going to have to work on this over and over again.

When you learn to focus and never *lose sight* of the goal you want to achieve, you'll discover the incredible power from the forces of the universe as divine providence assists you. So take the time to visualize in technicolour what it is you say you want. Learn to meditate upon your dreams and discover how solutions will come into your mind like autumn leaves falling to the ground. This requires a whole new discipline to *think* and not *do*. And yet even thinking is really an action. We just can't see it, unless smoke starts to drift out of your ears!

So make time to focus and never let go of your goals.

Ready! Aim! Fire!

The next focus area we addressed was that of setting and achieving goals. Transfer the intangible to paper and start making a tangible plan of action to see goals achieved. The goals setting process was compared with planning a family vacation. You have to know the *destination* you want to reach first. Then you work your way backwards to the beginning so you will know the *route* to take.

Eight suggested areas of one's life were proposed for you to hang your various goals under, and to try and ensure some semblance of balance in your life. Having several goals from different areas of your life also enables you to quickly move on to another goal should one area generate a failure. This helps maintain self-esteem, can provide learning for future experiences, and test your level of belief for wanting to really achieve this or another goal.

If You Build It...

Few of us have not seen the Kevin Costner film, *Field of Dreams* where Ray Kinsella knows without a shadow of a doubt that he has to build a baseball diamond in a cornfield. He also knows that he cannot ignore the soft, almost imperceptible command that *"if you build it, they will come."*

So where do you stand in the field of life with the writing out of your goals? Are you confident that you have all the dreams and longings written down? Do you have a picture of where you want to be five years from now? Is it written down? Do you look at it often? Are you prepared to build it so these goals will come about?

Action Stations!

As with anything worthwhile in life, all the planning in the world will not make your goals come about by themselves. Hopefully, you are already seeing how your Statement of Purpose affirmed in your mind acts as a driving force to get you moving towards action.

By working on the development of clear and meaningful plans to accomplish your goals, you will be even further motivated to step out and reach to the future. As the oft repeated Chinese proverb counsels us, *"the journey of a thousand miles begins with a single step."* So step out and up, and do it!

You should now have a master copy of your Strategic Life Plan. This will be your personal road map to the future. It will assist you to achieve your life purpose you have also written out. You will now begin to see your life's dreams become a living reality!

Planning Your Plan

One way to make your goals come alive is to use one of the many time management planners to its maximum usage. Depending on the size of your planner, you can enlarge or reduce a copy of your five year plan and put it in a section that is specifically set up for goal setting and achieving or create a section of your own.

The next thing to do is to narrow down the focus to your first year's goals. Break down all the steps and actions you are going to have to do to reach each of the goals identified under your first year. This will create some logical order to the goals that must be assigned to each respective month.

Most planners have some space on the monthly dividers for you to write down monthly goals, or just create your own sheet that you can insert with your goals for each month.

On a weekly basis, you review your monthly goals in light of the one year goal you want to reach to get you to year five. It's best to take the same day, same time, same place to do your goal setting each week. For me, Sunday as a day of rest allows me to reflect on my goals and the next steps to focus on my success.

From the weekly planning it's just a matter of slotting in the activities in your *to do* list section of your planner on the day you think it will best accomplished. You will discover that your goals get broken down into such small bite-size pieces, that working on your goals will begin to seem like fun. And as you achieve each small part of your goal, you check off your daily to-do list, mark items done on your weekly planning, your monthly and quarterly reviews, and before you know it a year has gone by. You will soon see the benefit of this discipline as you achieve each of your goals.

Not Carved In Stone

Some people have said that planning out their lives like this is just *too* much. They want to be spontaneous and enjoy life. Who wants to be controlled by a plan that you *have* to do?

It is very important to remember that your five year Strategic Life Plan is *not* carved in stone! It is written down on paper in either pen or pencil. No one is forcing you to plan your life. Neither are you obligated to work on one goal or another. But by having it written down you have luck on your side. For luck has been defined as preparation plus opportunity. By planning your life you are preparing for opportunity to knock on your door.

The minute you commit to reaching your goals, divine intervention comes into play with the laws of the universe to enlist the help of others in seeing your goals are achieved.

I have shared with you earlier how my own life has changed directions, just like the unusual twists and turns that happen on the highway of our life's journey. There will be detours along the way and sometimes a goal may have to be stopped or adapted because of one thing or another. You must be prepared to change directions. The ride will still be enjoyable. In fact, the scenery may end up being far more pleasant than you originally planned.

Yet when you are settled on your goals, and especially your more purpose driven goals, you have to commit to achieving them no matter what the cost in time, money or effort.

A promotion, an opportunity to move, a downsized layoff, marriage, a welcome birth, an unexpected death, a chance of a lifetime. All these experiences can influence you to rewrite your five-year plan. Each year you will rewrite your five year plan. You will see how far you have come in contrast with where you want to be. But some goals will never be changed because they are too important to you.

For myself, the one-time pursuit and goal of a Ph.D. in organizational psychology with all it's long-term projection of annual and monthly steps, was soon changed to professional speaking. All this came about as I received more and more requests to speak. And I also discovered the great reward of giving to others what I had found out about life. This necessitated a midstream course correction.

This has also been the case for me as I moved from part-time professional speaker to full-time, after a downsizing lay-off from a management position in the healthcare field. It gave me the kick-start I needed to get going.

One of the first things I had to do was to rewrite my goals. Funny enough, one of the goals was to go full-time with my business. It came sooner than I had planned. But I think it was easier to move into going full-time because it was already written down. I had expected to be there even if things had not worked out previously. I was confident that someday it would be achieved. I had seen it and I believed it, no matter how frustrated along the way I got with life's curve balls.

Opportunity Is Always Knocking

You too will see goals come to life when you least expected it. Somehow, by having written it down, by thinking on it often, reading it regularly, talking about it with close personal friends or your spouse, a door opens and beckons you to enter on an adventure you had not planned.

Remember, you are in control of your life and in doing your goals. You have by now hopefully written out your goals. It will be hard to ignore them. They will be like a magnet drawing you towards them. Like the sirens of mythology they will be the haunting voices from the sea calling out to you to start working on their achievement.

Your life purpose will help you in wanting to reach your goals. It will be your motivation to achieve the goals you have carved out for yourself. But they will not be carved in stone.

They will be etched out carefully and with pride and spirit into your mind and heart. This is no stone carving. This is one which is living, moving, and dynamic.

So you are not bound to the plan. You should not be so rigid that you are not spontaneous in your actions or in your life in general. You will find out an uncanny truth. With the structure of life planning comes the freedom to live the life you choose. Whatever you choose to be, your plan should be bound by your life purpose. This will determine the goals you will never sacrifice and the ones that life can change course for you.

Freedom and flexibility will carry over into how you prioritize your goals and how you work towards them. Some goals will lose their priority and may even fall from view of your life plan. Others will appear as if from nowhere and be added to the ranks of your Strategic Life Plan. Other more meaningful goals will always be staring at you, longing to be reached. All it takes is *action!*

Focus Points On Action

Point #1: Write down one thing you want to focus on in your life. Practice doing something each day until you see your focus area accomplished. Believe you can succeed.

Point #2: Make sure you know the difference between *like* and *love*. Whatever you say you want in life you must *love* it in order to be focused.

Point #3: To focus on your success start with your attitude. You obtain the right kind of attitude one thought at a time.

Point #4: Entertain successful thinking on a daily basis. When you entertain doubtful thinking it will steal the show.

Point #5: Remember that fear is a learned response. This makes it easy to conquer by simply asking others for help and learning one step at a time the skills to overcome your fear.

JUST ONE THING MORE

Belief is the seed and action is the nurturing, fertilizing power for your success. So here are some final action ideas to help you stay focused on success.

For quite a while I would write down on the journal/daily record page of my planner the words *"One Thing"* in red ink. Then I would write down just *one* thing that I must do that day to move me towards one of my major goals. Simply writing down these two words, boldly standing out from the black and blue ink on the rest of the page, helped me to *focus* on that one task. When achieved, I would tick off the box I had created for that item.

More recently I found I was successfully reaching these daily "one things". It was not as difficult to do as it once had been. I needed something more challenging.

I have shared with you that goal *setting* was fairly easy for me to do. My struggle has been with the doing, the self-discipline to stay focused on the goals. So I now review my monthly goals each day to see if there are some specific actions I should be doing that particular day. Instead of "one thing" written in red ink, I now have the word "goals" with the specific goals for that day written in red ink. The red ink has been a real attention grabber for me. I am becoming much more focused.

You must develop some way to always have your goals with you, whether it is in your planner, on 3" by 5" cards, a separate book all together. Keep them with you.

Your Personal Review

To really focus on success you have to focus on it every single day. Since your goals are the markers of success you want to achieve, you are going to have to review them every single day.

Personally, I manage to do this in the morning. Not only do I review my monthly goals and define what goals I need to achieve that day and write them down (in red pen, remember) in my planner, I also do an affirmation like exercise. This comes from Brian Tracy who suggests writing out your major focus goals in their positive, present tense as if they were always being achieved.

My goals that I write down every single day cover the various focus areas in the Strategic Life Plan. Many a time the goal statement of *"I am a positive, fun-loving father"* has helped me move away from actions that were opposite from that statement.

This has really helped me to review my major goals for this year on a daily basis. So along with the daily check of my monthly goals, I know I am moving further ahead than I have done in the past with my attempts at goal achieving.

Many of the great writers and speakers in motivation and goal setting, have suggested reading your goals, even out loud several times a day in the morning upon awakening and before retiring to bed. I have to acknowledge and admire the discipline and drive of these people as I am not yet there. Notice I said not *yet!* But *I will!*

The bottom line principle here is *you have to review your goals daily.* Period.

Whatever method you find works best for you, use it and make it work for you. The key is to use every one of your senses available to you. Every sensory input you can use will help make your goals come alive for you. You must be driven to achieve your goals.

Master-Mind Approach

One of the best things that happened to me to help get my goals really focused was when I met with my friend, Michael Schumacher, on a weekly basis to review our goals. We used this one hour of time to share successes and failures, review our goals for the past week, and set new goals for the week ahead.

There were times that the night before our meeting I would be working feverishly to accomplish an important goal by the next day. It's amazing what a little self-induced pressure will do to motivate us to do something.

Michael has moved since we first met so we no longer meet in person. But we still connect on the telephone or in person and go through the same process of reviewing our progress and challenging ourselves with new goals.

A Master-Mind is where two or more people get together to share knowledge and assist each other in reaching one another's goals. They hold a common purpose or interest.

Another MasterMind that I belong to is made up of myself and three other speakers in the city in which I live. Illoana Smith comes with a sales and marketing background with presentations on sales, networking, cold calling, and other topics. Diane Stewart also has a sales background, and presents sales and management training along with personal growth programs. Cindy Palajac has had a major focus with self-esteem, goal setting and wellness.

Together we all bring different strengths and talents to the monthly meetings. So far we have discussed marketing ideas, how to partner together, and have shared different leads. We have created joint marketing efforts and put on speakers showcases for meeting planners. One of the incredible benefits of such a MasterMind group is the support for one another and the genuine excitement and enthusiasm generated from each other's ideas.

Some thoughts to consider in creating your very own MasterMind group include:

MasterMind Checklist

1. Small is beautiful (4 to 6 is ideal; no more than 9)
2. Share a common purpose
3. Build upon trust and confidentiality
4. Obtain expert advice from each other
5. Act as a sounding board for each other's ideas
6. Exchange contacts and business leads
7. Rotate meeting leadership
8. Plan ahead for next meeting with a theme or question
9. Hold at least one retreat a year
10. Total commitment to group development

Heroes, Landmarks, & Treasures

One method to keep yourself focused on your goals and to get really excited about achieving them, is to obtain some tangible motivators. You can then draw on these items when time gets tough. They will physically remind you that you can do it.

Drawing upon the *heroes* of your life can be kind of exciting, especially when you take the time to write them, and more so when you get a chance to meet them in person.

Being in the speaking profession, I have had the chance to telephone, write, and meet with many speakers who are at the forefront of our profession. They are people who not only talk, they walk their talk. There is nothing worse than to have someone you look up to not living by the standards they profess to be living in the public spotlight.

I have made a list of many of my favourite authors and speakers that I want to meet during my lifetime. Some I never imagined I would get a chance to meet, and have had some unexpected encounters with a few that generated great discussions and memories.

Such moments will always stand out as being most memorable. Like seeing Og Mandino, the prolific and famous motivational author, for my second time while attending a convention, only to learn of his passing away just two months later. I am glad to have captured a memory with a photograph.

So make time to write a thank you letter to an author whose book has made a difference to you. I have done this a few times. The one I will treasure the most was writing Norman Vincent Peale and thanking him for his outstanding book, *The Power of Positive Thinking*, which so powerfully affected my life in my early teens.

Never did I expect to get the kind of reply that I did. Not only did Dr. Peale respond to my letter with sincere gratitude, but he sent me an autographed hardback copy of a subsequent book, *The Power of Positive Living*. Within a year, Norman Vincent Peale passed away, and I am ever so grateful that I was able to thank him for the difference he made in my life.

Make the time today to write someone well known who has affected your life. You will feel good as I did.

So make your list of the famous and notable people you would like to know, meet, or write. Now plan the many ways to reach your goal. It becomes ever so exciting to tick off alongside their names when you actually meet them.

Another way to recognize your own achievements is to generate a list of _landmarks_, places you've always wanted to go to that would spark the child-like spirit of adventure inside of you. It is especially meaningful if these landmark places can help you further your quest in achieving your goals.

Make sure when you are going to take your camera along and capture the memories of _"being there"_. Make up a photo album of not just the photographs but any of the memorabilia that can help you remember.

This can often coincide with meeting some of your heroes. One word of caution. Make sure you know how to use your camera. I had bought a new camera for my trip to the National Speakers Association Convention, and after capturing some shots of all the great speakers with myself, yes, I accidentally pressed the wrong button and popped open the camera losing my pictures.

After about 15 minutes reframing my feelings and attitudes, I said to myself, _"I'll just have to do this again sometime!"_. And I will.

Your Very Own Treasure Chest

Finally, is the collecting of _treasures_ that remind you of accomplishing your goals. Whether it is tangible objects like awards or plaques, or treasuring memories through meditating on the thoughts and images of an exceptional experience. Sometimes, we need to treasure all of the many feelings of competence, completion and confidence of our successes.

To help with remembering our successes, it is a good idea to write down five major accomplishments that you have done in your life and carry them around with you. I have mine on a 3" x 5" card that I had laminated. Just pull it out when you get discouraged or you are struggling with staying focused. Recall the feelings of those treasured successes and move forward with renewed vigor and enthusiasm.

By having a reservoir of experiences with your heroes, landmarks and treasures, you can let down your bucket when you run dry of the waters of motivation. This is a valuable wellspring and source of strength to keep you focused on the success you desire.

Keeping Score

If you play golf or any sport for that matter, why do you keep score? You want to know how well you have done. You will probably compare it with your previous performance. And it will probably help you know where you may need to improve your skills. So keeping score is an O.K. thing to do.

Imagine going to a bowling arena to play ten-pin bowling. This time though, the machinery is not working very well and the curtain of brushes is always blocking the view of the pins. The TV monitors are also not working.

After you throw the ball you hear that unmistakable sound of the falling pins, but you don't know if you shot one or all of them down. This would be a very frustrating evening if this was the way the whole game went. You would quickly lose motivation to keep playing.

Similarly, it is good to keep track of the score of your goal achievement to see how many "pins" you have knocked down, and see which ones you still have to shoot for. Your list of 101 goals maybe a good list to tick off, cross out, or highlight. Maybe you would like to use your Strategic Life Plan and put sticky stars next to the ones you have reached.

Knowing the score is for your own benefit and satisfaction in achieving your goals. *Never* boast your accomplishments to others. Doing so may affect the self-esteem of the other person and end up being *de*motivating. Those around you would far better benefit from what you have learned. Share your experiences and assist them in achieving their personal goals. That way, you *both* score.

Put On Your Walking Shoes

All along, the goal setting process has been likened to planning a journey. You look to where you want to be and work your way backwards to the present and figure out the actions you need to take today.

So when you get down to this year, you need to plan your *monthly marathon* and get yourself in shape to make sure each of the goals that you want to do are slotted into the month most likely to be achieved in. From running your marathon you can get your focus on success in shape by carrying out your *weekly walk*, which is a lot easier to manage and seems less out of your comfort zone. Which brings you back to your *daily single step* of just putting one step in front of the other. What is crucial about your single step is *action!*

If you want to make something of yourself, make a difference in whatever field of endeavour that you choose, and contribute something of lasting value to the people of the world....then you are going to have to move! Do. Do it. Do it now!

I'll never forget the time my uncles invited me down to their offices in one of the downtown skyscrapers of Toronto, Canada. I had just arrived from England, where I came from a small town in comparison with the metropolis I was going to. I was just turning 17 years of age and quite intimidated by the large city. I was unaware where to begin to get a job.

The one uncle called me into his office and was pleasant at first. Then he spoke some words to me that I would never have spoken being fresh from proper England. He told me to "get off your bum and get a job!"

Personally, I needed that kick in the pants. And within one month of arriving in Canada I had a job as a management trainee in a bank. The point is, I needed to move. Action was required. The job did not fall into my lap. I had to scout it out, prepare for it, and get it. All these steps add up to make a marathon winner.

You have taken some action steps in reading this book to this point. I hope that as you reflect on each of the focus areas you will do more than just read. You have got to believe you can find your success. You have got to create a determined and positive attitude to achieve success. You must set the goals that will lead you to the success you want. And then you are left with one thing to do. ACTION!

All of these things require that you *focus* your energy, your thoughts, your time, your passion, your drive, your body, your effort, and everything you have towards *your* definition of success.

Sailing To Success
With Relationships

At the same time, remember to keep a proper perspective and balance on the success you want to reach. Never chart your course towards the high seas of success without first checking out the condition of your relation-*ships*.

It is only as you focus on the people in your life, whether family, friends or business clients, that the real success will start to come to you. Never lose focus of the important people in your life.

A Final Reflection
On Focus

You and I have spent a fair bit of time together. Hopefully, by sharing the different experiences I have with you, you can see that when you lose focus you tend not to achieve what it is you want in life. As you work on the exercises throughout the book and review the focus points at the end of each chapter, you will be practicing an essential skill for reaching and achieving your goals.

The act of focusing on success is, I believe, an ongoing process for many of us. Some will be more adept than others. If you are one of these, share what you know with others, especially your children. Take time to teach as many individuals as you can before they lose focus and give up.

For many of you who have found the art and practice of focusing on success a challenge, stay with it and practice, practice, and practice some more. Focus every day on what you want to have, what you want to be, and what you want to do. Never give up. Stay focused.

How To Focus On Success!

Let me share some parting thoughts with you. Focusing on anything, whether by sight, hearing, touch, or in our minds, is not an easy task. You have to increase your awareness of what you're focusing on. You may have to acquire new knowledge and skills to be able to do this. It takes experience. Mostly, it is a state of mind.

As I examined my own life experiences I realized there were markers of success at different points in time. In writing them down, they looked like dots in a join-the-dot children's puzzle book. Somehow, there were long blanks in between with no success moments.

By doing some introspection I could see that the dots of success were when I was focused. The blanks? I discovered I had lost focus. In asking myself what steps I had taken when I was successful and focused, allowed me to discover the principles you have read in this book.

The most important principle to follow in focusing on success, is to *believe.* Every action you take each minute of your life, is done with belief that it will happen or be successful. This means you have to start exercising your thinking and your feeling towards any action you really want to achieve.

That is exactly how this book began. Merely a belief that all of us need to be more focused in life. And each day I had faith that I could write a page or two. Before I knew it a chapter was completed. In four months the first draft of the book was completed.

After editing and graphic design I had to find funding to self-publish the book. Marketing, publicity and distribution all had to be learned to get this book into your hands. All of these new experiences required belief to even begin. And the fruits have certainly been pleasing to me.

Stay Focused

Whatever areas in life you need to focus on will require you to develop many attributes: patience, determination, attentiveness, diligence, consistency, resilience, courage, and many others. You will need these qualities for yourself. You will need them when others tear you down for pursuing your dream. They are essential for staying focused.

Follow every step outlined in this book. Write down your goals. Believe you can do what it is you want to do. Develop a winning attitude by cleaning out the negatives and developing your focused mind. Build up the relationships with those you love and admire. And from the seedbed of faith, sow the seeds of action! You know you can do it. You have felt you can many times while reading this book.

So accept the challenge to reach your full potential. Decide today, if you haven't already, to personally make a difference in your personal life, in your family, business and community. Stay focused until the goal is reached. Fulfill your life purpose everyday.

With all the faith that I have, I pray that you will have the success that you desire and most of all deserve. All you need to do is *focus.*

Focus Points On Action

Point #1: You must practice getting out of your comfort zone if you want to move towards your focus point. Just staring at it won't see you reach your success.

Point #2: It takes just one thing a day to reach your goals. Imagine if you did more!

Point #3: Look at your goals everyday. Focus. Listen to your voice from within. What do you *feel* you have to work on? What do you *know* you should do? Now, go and do it.

Point #4: The Chinese proverb says, "many hands make light work". Many minds make ideas come alive. Start a Master Mind group today.

Point #5: Write a favourite hero. Visit a significant landmark. Polish a meaningful treasure. Stop and reflect on the success you already have through your treasure chest of life.

Point #6: Whether family, friend or client, take the time to say "thank you". Many a thank you card gets read again and again. Celebrate the success of others around you.

Point #7: Thank you for staying focused to the very last page of this book. May the *focus* be with you!

ABOUT ROY SAUNDERSON

Roy Saunderson is one of North America's leading experts in the art and science of giving effective recognition. As a keynote presenter, Roy is known for providing practical "nuts and bolts" for people to take away, as well as giving them the motivation to succeed. He is also a sought after trainer who makes sure his audiences feel like stars with his warm, captivating style and a message of genuine caring.

He is the founder of the Recognition Management Institute, a consulting and training company focused on showing people how to give recognition to others, and to themselves.

Roy addresses groups from professional associations, healthcare organizations, and leading corporations. His clients have included Alliance of Canadian Travel Associations, Bell Canada, Business Development Bank of Canada, Canada Post Corporation, Canadian Hospital Engineering Society, London Life Insurance, Oakville-Milton Real Estate Board, Ontario Hospital Association, Royal Bank of Canada, Union Gas, University of Western Ontario, and the Young President's Assistants.

For more information on Roy Saunderson's books, tapes, speaking and consulting services, or to schedule him for a presentation to your company or organization, contact:

Recognition Management Institute
635 Southdale Road East, Suite 180
London, Ontario CANADA N6E 3W6

Tel: (519) 685-0564 • Fax: (519) 685-0819

For additional copies of
How To Focus On Success!
visit your favourite bookstore.

For special orders and bulk purchases,
please call (519) 685-0564 or fax (519) 685-0819

ORDER FORM

Quantity	Price	Total

How To Focus On Success! Paperback

_____ $16.95 $ _____

Focus On Success 52 Mini-Posters (8 1/2 x 11)
of Inspirational Quotes

_____ $5.95 $ _____

Believing In The Magic Within You! Single Audiotape

_____ $11.95 $ _____

SUBTOTAL $ _____

7% Goods & Services Tax $ _____

8% Tax (Ontario Residents only) on **tapes & posters** only $ _____
Shipping and handling
($4.00 on first item; 50¢ each addl. item) $ _____

┌─────────────────────────────────┐
│ **QUANTITY DISCOUNTS**   **TOTAL $** _____
│ ARE AVAILABLE ON BULK PURCHASES
└─────────────────────────────────┘

_____

Name

_____(___)_____

Company   Phone #

_____

Address

_____

City   Province/State   Postal / Zip Code

_____

MasterCard or VISA #   Exp. Date

Cheques made payable to   _____
Recognition Management Institute Signature for all Credit Card orders
For more information about Roy Saunderson's speaking and consult-
ing services call: Recognition Management Institute, 635 Southdale
Rd. E., Ste. 180, London, Ontario Canada N6E 3W6;   (519) 685-0564.